The Woman in

A play by
Constance Cox

Adapted from the novel by
Wilkie Collins

Samuel French — London
New York - Toronto - Hollywood

Please see page iv for further copyright information

CHARACTERS

Mrs Vesey, the housekeeper, elderly
Walter Hartright, late 20s
Marion Halcombe, 25
Mr Gilmore, a solicitor, elderly
Mr Frederick Fairlie, middle-aged
Louis, his valet, Swiss
Laura Fairlie, Marion's half-sister, 20 ⎫ *played by the*
Anne Catherick, 20s ⎭ *same actress*
Sir Percival Glyde, 40
Count Fosco, middle-aged
Countess Fosco, middle-aged
Mrs Catherick, Anne's mother, middle-aged

SYNOPSIS OF SCENES

The action takes place in the drawing-room of Limmeridge Hall in Cumberland

Time —1861 and 1862

ACT I

SCENE 1 The drawing-room. July 1861. Evening
SCENE 2 The same, a month later. Early evening.

ACT II

SCENE 1 The same. November 1861. Afternoon.
SCENE 2 The same, two days later. Early evening.

ACT III

The same. March 1862. Early evening

COPYRIGHT INFORMATION

(See also page ii)

ACT I

SCENE 1

The drawing-room at Limmeridge Hall, Cumberland. July 1861

French windows in the back wall lead on to a terrace which overlooks the garden. Double doors UL (with a bellrope to their L) lead to the hall, and the major part of the house, and there is another door R. The room's furniture and hangings speak of wealth. There is a fireplace R, with a small chair and footwarmer DS of it, a mirror over it, and fire-irons and bellows. There is a clock on the mantelpiece. An armchair is set RC with a small table beside it. A sideboard with a lamp on it stands against the back wall R of the windows, with a screen between it and the windows. L of the windows and against the back wall is a desk with a chair in front of it and pens, an inkstand, notepaper, blotting paper, a lamp and two sketch-books on it. A sofa is angled at LC with a small table at the R end of it. An occasional table is against the wall DL, with a small chair slightly in front of it; also DL is a small footstool

When the CURTAIN *rises the windows that lead to the terrace are open, as are the curtains. A fire burns in the fireplace though the evening is warm*

Mrs Vesey, an elderly housekeeper, enters UL, speaking as she comes. She is followed by Walter Hartright, a young man in his late twenties

Mrs Vesey (*moving* C) And this is the drawing-room, Mr Hartright. We generally sit here of an evening, so I do hope you'll join us sometimes.

Hartright Will I be permitted, Mrs Vesey?

Mrs Vesey But of course! Mr Fairlie won't object, and the girls and I see so few new faces you'll be doing us a favour. Now, are you quite sure you won't rest before dinner? You've had such a long journey from London.

Hartright Quite sure, thank you. I'm not in the least tired.

Mrs Vesey Then you must take a glass of sherry and a biscuit. (*She moves to the sideboard and pours a glass of sherry during the following*)

Hartright You're very kind. (*He moves to the sofa*) Can you tell me if Mr Fairlie will see me tonight?

Mrs Vesey Oh, I couldn't say. You see, Mr Fairlie is such a sad invalid. But no doubt if he finds himself strong enough he will send for you. (*She places the glass of sherry and a plate of biscuits on the small table R of the sofa*) Now make yourself comfortable while I go and acquaint him of your arrival.

Hartright (*sitting on the sofa*) Have you any specimens of my pupils' work that I could see while I'm waiting?

Mrs Vesey Why, certainly. (*She fetches the two sketch-books from the desk*) Here is Miss Fairlie's sketch-book; you'll be pleased with that, Mr Hartright ... And — I'm afraid this is Marion's.

Hartright (*smiling*) Why afraid?

Mrs Vesey Marion is a dear girl, Mr Hartright, but she really only draws to keep Laura company.

Marion Halcombe enters through the french windows. She is a young woman of about twenty-five, of strong character and forthright speech

Marion (*moving* c) Mrs Vesey, did I hear the trap come back from the station? (*She sees Hartright*) Oh!

Hartright rises

Mrs Vesey Yes, this is Mr Hartright, dear. Miss Marion Halcombe, sir.

Marion Welcome to Limmeridge Hall, Mr Hartright. (*She holds out her hand*)

Hartright (*moving to Marion*) Thank you. (*He shakes her hand*)

Mrs Vesey I'm just going to your uncle, my dear, to tell him Mr Hartright has arrived.

Mrs Vesey exits UL

Hartright I've just been looking at your sketches, Miss Halcombe. (*He moves back to the sofa, and picks up the books*)

Marion Oh, dear! (*Laughing*) Well, at all events, you know the worst about me.

Hartright I dare say your talents lie in another direction.

Marion Do you? Then I wish you'd tell me where, for I can't find them. (*She sits* R)

Hartright The piano?

Marion No.

Hartright Then — needlework, perhaps?

Marion No.

Hartright Well — er ...

Marion (*laughing*) You're determined to be polite, Mr Hartright, but it's no use. Let's face the fact: I'm an unaccomplished woman.

They laugh together

Now forget about me and look at my sister's drawings. *She* really is clever enough to repay your tuition.

Hartright (*surprised*) Is Miss Fairlie your *sister?*

Marion Yes. (*She understands his perplexity*) Oh, I see, you're wondering about the name. My mother was married twice. First to Mr Halcombe, my father. Then to Mr Philip Fairlie — *this* Mr Fairlie's brother.

Hartright I see. So you and Miss Fairlie are really half-sisters. (*He puts the sketch-books down on the table* DL)

Marion That's right. Only Laura's father died rich and mine didn't, so she's an heiress and I'm penniless. However, on his brother's death Mr Frederick Fairlie was persuaded to take charge of us both, which is why you find me in this great house in spite of my poverty.

Hartright That was very good of Mr Fairlie.

Marion Yes — perhaps. Well, now that you know all about us, suppose you tell me something about yourself. How did my uncle persuade you to give up all your pupils, and bury yourself for three months in the wilds of Cumberland?

Hartright (*sitting on the sofa*) Most of my pupils are away for the summer, and I was very glad of the employment. But even if I hadn't needed it I think …

Marion (*after a pause*) Yes?

Hartright I think curiosity would have brought me here.

Marion Curiosity? To see my uncle's art collection, do you mean? It is considered very fine.

Hartright No, not that. Because of an experience I had in London.

Marion Oh?

Hartright I heard this house and your mother's name mentioned in the most extraordinary circumstances.

Marion But my mother has been dead for years!

Hartright I know.

Marion You know?

Hartright (*nodding*) I also know she did much good here. Amongst other things she founded the village school.

Marion (*astonished*) Have you been in this part of Cumberland before?

Hartright No. I learnt all this in London — or, to be more exact, on the *road* to London.

Marion The road?

Hartright It was just before I came here — very late at night. I'd been spending the evening with some friends and I was walking home. All of a sudden I heard a step behind me — then there was a touch on my shoulder. I turned round — and before me stood a woman — dressed from head to foot in white!

Marion You mean — her bonnet, dress and everything?

Hartright Yes. For a moment I thought she was a ghost. Then she said,"Is this the road to London?"

Marion What kind of a woman was she? Was she young?

Hartright Yes — not more than twenty at the most. She would have been pretty if she hadn't looked so ill — and so dreadfully frightened.

Marion Go on, Mr Hartright. What happened then?

Hartright I assured her she was on the road to London, and we began to walk along together ...

Marion Did she speak again?

Hartright Not for some time. She kept glancing over her shoulder, as if she were afraid of being followed. Then, quite suddenly, she asked me a most curious question.

Marion What?

Hartright She asked — it so astonished me I had to make her repeat it. She asked if I knew many men of rank and title.

Marion How extraordinary. What did you say?

Hartright I told her I had met a few, and asked her why she wished to know. "Because", she said, "there is one — a baronet — I hope you will never, never meet."

Marion A baronet? Did she tell you his name?

Hartright I asked her, naturally. But — "I can't — I daren't tell you," she said. "I forget myself when I speak of him." Then, as we were now on the outskirts of London, she asked me abruptly if I would get a cab for her.

Marion Had she told you where she was going?

Hartright No, and I didn't like to question her. But just before the cab drove off, she asked me if I lived in London. It occurred to me that she might be thinking of applying to me for help. So I felt bound to tell her I was taking up a temporary position in Cumberland.

Marion And it was then that she mentioned my mother?

Hartright Yes.

Marion And spoke of the school she founded and this house?

Hartright Yes.

Marion What was she like — apart from being dressed all in white?

Hartright Young, as I said. Slight — pretty, fair hair.

Marion But it was dark. You never really saw her clearly?

Hartright I saw her face once — by the lights of the cab. I shall never forget it ... It was so unhappy.

Marion And that was the end of your adventure when she drove off in the cab?

Hartright Not quite the end. (*He rises and moves* L) Something more happened.

Marion What?

Hartright I'd barely reached the ——

Mrs Vesey enters quickly UL *and comes* C

Mrs Vesey Oh, Mr Hartright, Mr Fairlie wishes to see you. He's coming right away.
Marion (*rising*) Not here, surely?
Mrs Vesey Yes, dear, so you'd better go. (*She moves to the fireplace*) You know how he dislikes a crowd. (*She blows up the fire with the bellows*)
Marion (*moving* UC) I'll come back later, Mr Hartright. I must hear the end of this.

Marion exits R

Mrs Vesey Oblige me by shutting the windows tight, Mr Hartright.

Hartright moves to the windows and closes them

Mrs Vesey Oh, and the curtains drawn, if you please.
Hartright The curtains *drawn*?
Mrs Vesey Mr Fairlie cannot stand a glare of any kind.

Hartright closes the curtains

Thank you so much. Now where did I put that foot-warmer? Ah, here it is. (*She finds it near the fireplace*)
Hartright A footwarmer in July?
Mrs Vesey Mr Fairlie feels the cold exceedingly. Now, if you'd be so good as to draw that screen forward to exclude the draught …

Hartright moves the screen in front of the windows

Thank you, thank you.

The door UL *opens and Louis, a Swiss servant, enters carrying a fumigating spray. He gravely examines the footwarmer, the fire and the curtains, then proceeds to fumigate the room with the spray*

Hartright watches in astonishment

Louis puts down the spray and goes out again UL

Mr Fairlie (*off*) Is the room fumigated, Louis?
Louis (*off*) Yes, m'sieur.
Mr Fairlie (*off*) Are the curtains drawn?
Louis (*off*) Yes, m'sieur.
Mr Fairlie (*off*) You're quite sure there are no draughts?
Louis (*off*) None, m'sieur.
Mr Fairlie (*off*) Have you my smelling salts and my eau-de-Cologne?

Louis (*off*) Yes, m'sieur.
Mr Fairlie (*off*) Then you may take me in.

Louis appears, wheeling Mr Fairlie in an invalid chair. Mr Fairlie, who is middle-aged and extremely well-preserved, is a perfect example of the imaginary invalid. A shawl is round his shoulders and a rug over his knees. A portfolio of drawings is by his side in the chair, as is a fan. During the following preparations he lies back with his eyes closed. Louis pushes him c then adjusts the screen between his chair and the door, then produces and holds out a box of lozenges to Mr Fairlie, who takes one

Hartright (*unable to bear the silence any longer; moving* DC) I would like to thank you, Mr Fairlie, for the generous way in which I've been welcomed. I hope I ——
Mr Fairlie (*interrupting; holding up his hand*) Are you Mr Hartright?
Hartright Yes.
Mr Fairlie Then would you be so kind as to speak a trifle less heartily? The slightest sound goes through my head like a knife.
Hartright I beg your pardon. As I was saying, I ——
Mr Fairlie (*holding up his hand again*) Would you mind standing a little further off? Germs fly to me, you know. Positively fly to me.

Hartright moves away to stand in front of the armchair

Thank you. Forgive me for not shaking hands with you, but I never touch anybody — not even my nieces. You won't mind if I occasionally close my eyes, will you? The fatigue — coming from my own apartments — all those corridors ——
Hartright I'm sorry you went to so much trouble. I could easily have come to you.
Mr Fairlie Ah, but my apartments have been fumigated, and you've just come from a train. I don't hold that against you, Mr Hartright ——
Hartright I should have found it difficult to come to Cumberland otherwise.
Mr Fairlie Quite, quite, I appreciate that. But in my experience I've found there is no place so germ-laden as a train, and as I said before, germs simply fly to me. Mrs Vesey ——
Mrs Vesey (*moving* DR *and curtsying*) Mr Fairlie?
Mr Fairlie I can hear you breathing. Go away.

Mrs Vesey moves between Hartright and Fairlie and exits UL

Hartright (*ironically*) Does *my* respiration offend you, Mr Fairlie?
Mr Fairlie Yes, exceedingly. But as I have to speak with you I must bear with it.

Hartright controls his feelings

Kindly make it as gentle as you can. Now to business. As I explained in my letter, I wish you — in the intervals of instructing my nieces in drawing and painting — to repair and mount some valuable water-colours I purchased recently. You may know I have something of a reputation as a collector.

Hartright nods

I am a wretched invalid, of course, but one must do what one can to imbue a vulgar world with an appreciation of beauty. Louis, the portfolio!

Louis takes the portfolio from the side of the chair

You may sit down, Mr Hartright.

Hartright sits in the armchair

Ah, don't move the chair! It may scroop! Hand that to Mr Hartright, Louis.

Louis hands the portfolio to Hartright, then returns to stand behind Mr Fairlie's chair

Pray give me your opinion of them, Mr Hartright.

Hartright (*looking in the portfolio*) Some of them have been badly misused, but I'm sure I can restore them. (*With enthusiasm*) They're superb examples, Mr Fairlie. I do congratulate you on having acquired them, and ——

Mr Fairlie (*holding up his hand*) Listen!

Hartright I beg your pardon?

Mr Fairlie I'm sure I heard some horrid children in the garden.

Hartright I heard nothing.

Mr Fairlie Possibly not. You were talking. Kindly oblige me by making sure.

Hartright rises, goes to the french windows, and opens the curtains during the following

There are no children in the house, but sometimes the servants encourage the brats from the village. Ah, be careful! The light!

Louis holds the fan before Mr Fairlie's eyes as Hartright looks out

Hartright (*closing the curtains and moving* R) The garden is quite empty, Mr Fairlie. (*He glances again at the portfolio*)

Mr Fairlie Thank you. My poor nerves, I suppose.

The door UL *opens and Laura Fairlie enters. She is about twenty, gentle and lovely*

Now who is that? I can feel a draught round the door!

Laura (*moving* C) It's me, uncle. Laura. I came to make myself known to Mr Hartright.

Mr Fairlie Really? I should have thought there was plenty of time for that. However, as you're here …. This is my niece Laura Fairlie, Mr Hartright. Give her plenty of paper to spoil and keep her out of my way.

Hartright looks up from the portfolio and sees Laura. The portfolio slips from his hands to the floor and he stands staring at Laura

Mr Fairlie (*of the crash of the falling portfolio*) Oh, dear. I knew that would happen. How very clumsy of you, Mr Hartright. My poor head!

Hartright I beg your pardon. (*He picks up the portfolio*)

Laura (*holding out her hand*) How do you do, Mr Hartright.

Hartright moves to her and takes her hand, still looking at her

Mr Fairlie Now there are so many people in the room my strength is going. You can manage the work then, Mr Hartright? Mr Hartright!

Hartright (*pulling himself together and moving* DR) It will be a pleasure to undertake it, Mr Fairlie. I shall perform it to the best of my ability.

Mr Fairlie Thank you. Yes would have been sufficient. Would you like Louis to carry that portfolio to your room?

Hartright Thank you. I can manage it myself.

Mr Fairlie Can you really? How delightful to be so strong.

Louis prepares to take Mr Fairlie out

I hope you'll enjoy your stay at Limmeridge Hall. Unfortunately, I shall have to deny myself the pleasure of your company, but you see what a sorry state I am in.

Louis turns the chair. Hartright puts the portfolio on the desk and opens the door UL

Thank you so much. You won't bang the door after me, will you? So kind of you to come all this way. Good-evening, Mr Hartright. Good-evening.

Mr Fairlie and Louis exit

Laura opens the curtains. Hartright moves the screen L

Laura I'm sorry my uncle was rude to you, Mr Hartright, but he's the same to everybody.

Hartright (*smiling*) I could forgive much more in anyone who gave me the chance to handle such treasures.

Laura Which of the water-colours has he given you to restore?

Hartright (*going to the portfolio*) These. The John Cromes.

Laura Oh, they're beautiful! (*She joins Hartright by the desk*)

Hartright Aren't they?

Laura (*looking at him, smiling*) What a fortunate man you are, Mr Hartright.

Hartright (*smiling back*) Am I? In what way?

Laura You are able to make what you love your work. And you *do* love your work. I can tell that from the way you handle those beautiful things.

Hartright Yes, that's true.

Laura How I envy you men! To be able to choose your professions — to go where you please — unhampered and free of control.

Hartright (*smiling*) We still have to work, you know. And the work isn't always as congenial as this.

Laura No, but ... (*She moves to the armchair*) Oh, it's no use ... I can't express it. Forgive me if I sounded stupid.

Hartright (*following her*) I think I know what you mean.

There is an immediate attraction between them of which both are conscious

Laura How long will you be staying?

Hartright Three months.

Laura Oh — then you'll be gone before I go.

Hartright Go? Are you leaving Limmeridge Hall?

Laura Yes. (*She moves* DR *with sudden reticence*) In the autumn.

A gong sounds, off

That's the dressing gong. I must go and change. (*She moves to the door* R)

Gilmore (*off; briskly*) I don't care if he's dying!

Mr Gilmore, an elderly and fiery solicitor, enters UL *followed by Mrs Vesey*

He's got to see me tonight! Ah, Laura, my dear.

Laura Good-evening, Mr Gilmore. Are you staying to dinner?

Laura and Gilmore shake hands

Gilmore I might — if that uncle of yours doesn't take away my appetite. Got to get that settlement of yours made out, you know. No time to lose.
Laura No ... I suppose not.

Laura glances at Hartright momentarily and exits R

Gilmore (*looking after Laura; to Mrs Vesey*) Well, go and tell him!
Mrs Vesey Couldn't it wait till after dinner, Mr Gilmore? Mr Fairlie says that if he discusses law before dinner, it gives him indigestion.
Gilmore You go and tell him if he doesn't see me now, I'll slam every door in the house and give him palpitations! Go on! Go on!

Gilmore pushes Mrs Vesey out of the door UL

Phew! The room stinks of him! (*He sees Hartright*) I beg your pardon. Staying here?
Hartright (*smiling*) Not exactly. I'm the new drawing master. My name's Hartright — Walter Hartright. (*He moves to Gilmore*)

Hartright and Gilmore shake hands

Gilmore Gilmore. Chancery Lane. Here to do some legal business for the family. Do you play chess?
Hartright (*startled*) Yes — as a matter of fact, I do.
Gilmore Shake hands again. It's a pleasure to meet a civilized man in this house. You must come and give me a game at my inn, while I'm forced to remain in this benighted country.
Hartright Doesn't Mr Fairlie play?
Gilmore Fairlie! (*He sits on the sofa*) Don't talk to me about him! I tell you, Mr Hartright, this house hasn't been the same since the other Mr Fairlie died.
Hartright There've been some changes since his time, I suppose?
Gilmore Changes! You may well say so. Time was when you could meet every family in the county in this drawing-room. Philip Fairlie was a man — not a fossilized mummy like his brother. Yes, there used to be some characters meet here, I can tell you. Old Joshua Wansborough, the magistrate — Andrew Weldon, who kept the village school ——
Hartright (*eagerly*) Would that be the school Mrs Fairlie founded?
Gilmore Why, yes, I think it was. What makes you ask?
Hartright I'm interested in it, that's all. (*He sits in the armchair*) Do you think it would be possible for me to see this Mr Weldon?
Gilmore I shouldn't advise you to try. He's been dead eleven years.
Hartright Oh.

Gilmore What's your interest in him?

Hartright I was — hoping to trace a pupil of his.

Gilmore No, afraid I can't help you there. Death's taken his toll pretty freely amongst us, Mr Hartright. Poor old Andrew! I'd like a sovereign for every quarrel I've listened to between him and Joshua Wansborough, when Josh had been riding his hobby horse a bit too hard. Josh had the strangest hobby you'd meet in a day's march.

Hartright Oh. What was it?

Gilmore (*rising*) Copying the Marriage Register of the Parish Church. (*He moves to the french windows*) The church you can see from here. Old Welmington.

Hartright (*rising*) What a curious hobby! (*He follows Gilmore to the windows*)

Gilmore I tell you, he was a character. "You can laugh", he used to say to us, "but the register's not safe lying about the vestry the way it is. Supposing there was a fire, or you wanted to check the date of a marriage. Then you'd thank me." And he kept that copy up-to-date for thirty-five years.

Hartright And did anyone ever use it?

Gilmore No, and there was never a fire. (*He produces a snuff box and taps it*) Poor old Joshua! All that effort and work for nothing! (*He takes snuff noisily*)

Hartright What happened to his labour of love?

Gilmore Heaven knows! Buried in the dust somewhere, I suppose.

Mrs Vesey enters UL *carrying a pair of slippers*

Well, can the poor suffering invalid see me?

Mrs Vesey Mr Fairlie is very low. I wish he were ten feet lower! Does he think his niece can get married without a proper settlement?

Hartright reacts to this

(*To Gilmore*) He says he'll see you if you put on these slippers so as to make no noise.

Gilmore Slippers! I'll be hanged if I will! He'll see me shod as I am and like it! Slippers, indeed! What does the man think he is? A Hindu temple!

Gilmore stamps out UL

Mrs Vesey But he expressly said ——

A door slams, off

Oh dear, oh dear!

Hartright (*crossing to Mrs Vesey*) Mrs Vesey — did Mr Gilmore say Miss
   Halcombe was to be married?
Mrs Vesey Not Miss Halcombe. Miss Fairlie.
Hartright Miss Fairlie! In the autumn?
Mrs Vesey Yes, to Sir Percival Glyde. Such a delightful gentleman. He's
   coming to stay next month, so you'll be able to meet him.

Marion enters UL, *a letter in her hand*

Another door slams, further off

   Marion, do you hear Mr Gilmore? I believe he does it on purpose. Oh, dear,
   oh, dear!

Mrs Vesey hurries off UL

Marion (*moving to Hartright*) Mr Hartright. I want you to look at this. It's
   an old letter of my mother's, written twelve years ago. (*She hands him the
   top sheet*) Read it.
Hartright (*moving* DR, *reading*) "We have a new pupil at the school, dear
   Philip ——"
Marion Laura's father.
Hartright "— and I have taken a violent fancy to her. (*He sits in the chair
   DR*) The poor little thing's intellect is not as developed as it should be at her
   age, but I have every hope of remedying that."
Marion You said the woman you met on the high road was young?
Hartright Twenty. Perhaps younger.
Marion Now see what it says further.
Hartright "I arranged yesterday that some of Laura's old white frocks and
   hats should be altered for little Anne Catherick, explaining to her that little
   girls of her age and complexion looked better in white than anything else
   …" Miss Halcombe!
Marion Go on!
Hartright "Her little hand clasped mine and she said, 'I will wear white as
   long as I live, dear Mrs Fairlie. It will help me to remember your goodness
   when I go away and see you no more.'" Then the woman I met on the road
   was ——
Marion Anne Catherick!
Hartright Have you the rest of the letter?
Marion Yes. Listen to this. I think it will surprise you. (*Reading from the
   second sheet*) "Now for the real reason for my fondness for little Anne
   Catherick. Although she is not half so pretty, she is, nevertheless …"

Hartright rises, slowly

   What is it?

Hartright I think I know what is coming next. But go on.

Marion (*reading*) "She is, nevertheless, in her complexion, the colour of her hair and eyes, the living, speaking likeness of my own dear Laura." (*She lowers the letter*)

Laura, in a white dress, appears on the terrace outside, looking across the garden, her profile to those inside. Hartright sees her, Marion does not

Hartright (*looking towards Laura*) Yes … It's true … They are horribly alike.

Marion Why do you say horribly? There's nothing dreadful in an accidental resemblance.

Hartright I never told you the sequel to my meeting with Anne Catherick, Miss Halcombe.

Laura moves out of sight along the terrace

Marion Sequel?

Hartright Not ten minutes after she left me, a carriage drove past me at a furious speed. It pulled up just ahead. Then a man jumped out and approached a constable on patrol … He asked if a woman dressed all in white had passed that way.

Marion Why did he want her? Did you hear?

Hartright Yes. She had escaped from — an asylum.

Marion An asylum! The poor, poor thing! (*She sits in the chair* DL)

Hartright (*moving to her*) I'm glad I helped her, but I can't bear to think of any association, however remote, between that helpless, sickly, frightened creature and Miss Fairlie. The one seems to cast a shadow over the future of the other.

Marion You're being fanciful, Mr Hartright. Laura has a brilliant marriage and future before her.

Hartright With someone she loves?

Marion (*with slight reproof*) With someone she respects.

Hartright I beg your pardon. I had no right to ask.

Laura reappears on the terrace

Please don't tell her what we've discovered

Laura enters, coming to the table at the end of the sofa. She is surprised at the expressions of Marion and Hartright

Laura (*smiling*) Is anything the matter? You look like a couple of conspirators.

Marion (*rising, startled*) Why are you wearing white, Laura? You never do.
Laura You say that as if you don't like it. Don't you like white, either, Mr
  Hartright?
Hartright Yes — yes, of course.
Laura Then I'm glad I've pleased one of you.

A gong sounds, off

Let me show you the way, Mr Hartright.

Hartright offers Laura his arm, and they exit through the door UL

*Marion looks at the letter in her hand, then, with a shrug, tears it across and
drops the pieces into the fire. She moves to the door* UL *as ——*

—— the CURTAIN *falls*

SCENE 2

The same, a month later. Early evening

When the CURTAIN *rises Hartright is sitting at the desk working on a drawing.
The light outside fades slowly during the scene*

After a moment Mrs Vesey enters R

Mrs Vesey Why, Mr Hartright, you'll strain your eyes! It's almost dark.
Hartright So it is.

Mrs Vesey lights the lamp on the sideboard

Can I help you with those? (*He rises*)
Mrs Vesey Thank you, if you would.

Hartright lights the desk lamp

I was so surprised when the young ladies came back from their drive alone.
I thought you'd gone with them.
Hartright No.
Mrs Vesey But you haven't been out with them at all this week, and you used
  to enjoy it so much. You mustn't work too hard, Mr Hartright. All work and
  no play, you know. (*She mends the fire, then closes the curtains*)
Hartright Mrs Vesey — do you think Mr Fairlie would see me for a few
  minutes tonight?

Mrs Vesey I don't know, I'm sure. Is it very important?
Hartright Very.
Mrs Vesey Then I'll see what I can do. (*She rises and moves near him*) Mr
Hartright ——
Hartright Yes?
Mrs Vesey It isn't my business, I know, but you haven't seemed very happy
these past two weeks. Is anything the matter? Is there anything I can do?
Hartright There's nothing you can do, Mrs Vesey, but thank you all the
same.
Mrs Vesey Well, if ever I can ... (*She moves up to the desk and sees his work*)
Oh, what a pretty drawing! It's Old Welmington Church! How clever you
are! (*She picks up the drawing*)
Hartright It's a little wedding gift for Miss Fairlie.
Mrs Vesey Oh, how kind of you! She'll love it. It's quite beautiful. (*She puts
the picture back on the desk*)
Hartright Thank you.
Mrs Vesey I'll speak to Mr Fairlie now. (*She moves to the door* UL *then turns*)
And, Mr Hartright, I do hope you'll join us after dinner tonight, and not go
up to your room again. We've missed your company sadly.

Mrs Vesey exits

*Hartright takes up his drawing and looks at it. The handle of the terrace
window is tried gently. He notices nothing. Then he takes the drawing to the
mantelpiece, places it upon it and stands back to look at it. The handle moves
again. This time he hears it and looks round. The window begins to open
slowly. Hartright moves swiftly to the corner* UR *and presses himself against
the wall*

*A hand parts the curtains, and Anne Catherick, dressed all in white, enters
timidly. She is the exact counterpart of Laura, but looks pale and ill. She
carries a letter in her hand*

*Anne moves softly towards the table by the sofa, and is about to lay the letter
down, when Hartright moves and shuts the window. She spins round,
terrified, a gasp escaping her, her body bent with fear. She looks all round
and takes a few steps, backing* DL, *trying to escape*

Hartright (*moving* C) Don't be frightened. I won't harm you, Miss
Catherick.

Anne gasps

That is your name, isn't it?

Anne (*whispering*) How do you know my name?
Hartright Don't you remember me? We've met before.

Anne shakes her head

Yes, we have — on the road to London.
Anne The road — to London?
Hartright We walked quite a way together.
Anne Oh, yes. I do remember now. You were very kind to me. (*Quickly*) You won't betray me now?
Hartright What are you doing here?
Anne I came because I saw it in the newspaper — I wanted to warn dear Mrs Fairlie's daughter.
Hartright Warn Miss Fairlie? (*He moves closer to Anne*) Against what?
Anne Against — never mind. (*She breaks* DL)
Hartright Won't you trust me, Miss Catherick? After all, I did help you to escape.
Anne (*gasping, moving behind the sofa, retreating from Hartright*) You know — about that?
Hartright I know where you'd run away from.
Anne (*moving* C) I'm not mad — truly I'm not! I've been very frightened — it was so awful in there. Promise you won't tell them that you've seen me?
Hartright I give you my word. (*Moving to her*) Now won't you tell me what you came to warn Miss Fairlie about?

Anne looks all round the room

Anne (*whispering*) Is it true she is to marry — *him*?
Hartright Sir Percival Glyde, do you mean? Yes, it's true.
Anne (*drawing a long, shuddering breath*) Oh, no!
Hartright What's it to you?

Anne retreats from Hartright DR. *He follows*

Miss Catherick, I'm Miss Fairlie's friend as well as yours. Can't you tell me?
Anne No, I dare not. But ——
Hartright Yes?
Anne If you will give her this. (*She makes to hand over the letter, then draws it back again*) You won't say that it came from me?
Hartright Providing you assure me that it contains nothing that will distress Miss Fairlie.
Anne It will help her — really it will. Please give it to her.

Hartright Very well. (*He takes the letter*)
Anne Thank you. (*She runs to the french windows*)
Hartright Miss Catherick ——

Anne stops

— is there no-one who can be of help to *you*? Have you no friends or relatives? Isn't your mother living?
Anne (*fiercely*) My mother? Yes, she's living! But she hates me. She called me an idiot. I'm not an idiot. I know what people say as well as anyone. That's why they put me away.
Hartright *They?* Your mother and who else?

Anne makes to speak, then changes her mind and slips out through the window. She disappears from view

(*Stepping out after her; calling*) Miss Catherick!

There is no reply. Hartright turns back into the room and looks at the letter in his hand

Marion enters UL

Marion Was someone here? I thought I heard voices.
Hartright You did. Anne Catherick has been here.
Marion Anne Catherick *here*? (*She moves to Hartright*) What did she want?
Hartright She gave me this letter for Miss Fairlie.
Marion Laura? Why should she write to her?
Hartright She said she wished to warn her. (*He hands her the letter*)
Marion Against whom?
Hartright I understood her to mean — the man Miss Fairlie is to marry.
Marion Sir Percival Glyde?

Hartright nods

But, surely ——
Hartright That was what she said.
Marion (*after a moment of perplexity*) Mr Hartright, I'm going to open this letter. I won't have Laura worried. If it contains nothing but the ravings of a deranged mind, there's no need for Laura to see it.
Hartright I think Anne Catherick knows very well what she's saying.
Marion Nevertheless … (*She opens the letter and reads it*) Oh, this is infamous! Infamous! Read it, Mr Hartright. (*She hands him the letter*)

Hartright reads the letter during the following

I never heard anything so abominable!
Hartright (*looking up*) There are no names mentioned. Does this description fit Sir Percival Glyde?
Marion Yes. There's no doubt she means it for him.

Hartright returns to the letter, finishes it and looks up

Well?
Hartright Shall you do as Anne Catherick suggests? Advise Miss Fairlie to enquire into his past life before she marries him?
Marion (*snatching the letter back*) You don't know what you say, Mr Hartright. There are not the slightest grounds for these insinuations. I've never heard a word against him. He was born in this very county — his parents were Mr Fairlie's dearest friends. He himself lived in Welmington until their death.
Hartright How long ago was that?
Marion Twenty — twenty-five years.
Hartright Then you know nothing of his mode of life since?
Marion (*turning on him angrily*) If there had ever been a breath of scandal against him, don't you think it would have reached us here?
Hartright There are things which are not made public.
Marion You believe this letter, don't you?
Hartright (*after a hesitation*) I know Anne Catherick well enough to know she does not lie.
Marion Very well. Then Sir Percival shall explain it himself. (*She pulls on the bell cord*)
Hartright You mean to send it to him?
Marion That won't be necessary. He arrived half an hour ago.

Mrs Vesey enters UL

Mrs Vesey, be so good as to ask Sir Percival to step here for a moment.
Mrs Vesey I think he's with Mr Fairlie, Marion.

Hartright crosses to the fireplace

Marion Never mind. This is more important than Mr Fairlie.
Mrs Vesey Very well, dear. Oh, and Mr Fairlie will see you in ten minutes, Mr Hartright.
Hartright Thank you.

Mrs Vesey moves to the door

Marion Wait! Ask Laura to come here, too.
Mrs Vesey Yes, dear.

Mrs Vesey exits

Hartright Is it wise to drag Miss Fairlie into this?
Marion Why not? (*She moves to him*) Don't you think she should hear her
   future husband vindicate himself? Or perhaps you think he won't?

Hartright is silent

   Mr Hartright, what is the matter with you? You seem determined to
   condemn somebody you don't even know on the unsupported statements
   of a woman whose mind, to say the least, is unstable.
Hartright I beg your pardon. I have Miss Fairlie's welfare at heart, too —
   more perhaps than befits my position.
Marion (*after a moment*) So that is why you've been avoiding us?
Hartright I'm asking Mr Fairlie to release me from the rest of my
   engagement. If he will, I shall leave tomorrow morning.
Marion I'm very sorry this has happened, Mr Hartright. I wish I could offer
   you some word of comfort. But you must see for yourself how hopeless it
   is.
Hartright I know, she's a wealthy woman and I'm — well — what I am.
Marion The difference of fortune would never matter to Laura, but hers is
   an engagement of honour — if not of love. It was her father's dearest wish
   that she should marry the son of his great friend, and unless the engagement
   is terminated by mutual consent, I can hold out no hope for you.

Sir Percival Glyde enters UL. *He is a handsome man of forty with a
charming easy manner*

Glyde (*moving* C) Ah, Miss Halcombe, you were inquiring for me, I believe?
Marion Yes, Sir Percival. Oh, you haven't met Mr Hartright, have you? Mr
   Hartright, this is Sir Percival Glyde.

Hartright and Glyde shake hands

Glyde How do you do, Mr Hartright. I've been seeing some of your work.
   Most excellent.
Hartright Thank you.
Glyde If you'd allow me to take some specimens with me to Italy. I believe
   I could put some commissions in your way.
Hartright You live in Italy?

Glyde (*smiling*) Alas, no — in Hampshire. My estate there, Blackwater Park. But we shall be spending the honeymoon in Naples with my greatest friend Count Fosco, and afterwards, he and his wife are returning with us to England. But perhaps you don't know of my good fortune, Mr Hartright? My marriage, I mean.

Hartright Yes … I do know of it. My — congratulations.

Glyde Thank you.

Laura enters UL

(*Moving to Laura and taking her hand*) Laura, my dear, did you know I've been in this house for half an hour without seeing you?

Laura (*withdrawing her hand*) I'm sorry. Mr Gilmore kept me. You wanted me, Marion? (*She moves to Marion*)

Marion Yes. Laura, this anonymous letter was left here for you. I opened it because I feared it might distress you. Now I think you should see it.

Laura takes the letter

Glyde (*strolling to the mantelpiece*) My dear Miss Halcombe, you sound extraordinarily serious.

Marion I am serious. Read it, Laura.

Laura sits on the sofa

Glyde (*picking up the drawing*) Old Welmington Church. Do you think it worth your pains, Mr Hartright?

Hartright Don't you? The architecture is interesting.

Glyde I think it an eyesore! I wish to heaven they'd pull it down!

Hartright looks surprised at his vehemence

(*Smiling at Hartright's reaction*) You'll gather I don't like Old Welmington, Mr Hartright. I don't. With all respect to these charming ladies, I think it the dullest place God ever made.

Laura (*looking up from the letter*) Marion, I don't understand this.

Marion Give it to Sir Percival. (*She sits on the chair* DL) He may be able to explain it.

Glyde I?

Laura hands Glyde the letter

May I? It's addressed to you.

Laura I want you to read it. I think it refers to you.

Glyde Indeed? (*He quickly reads a little of the letter*) Yes, you're right. This is obviously meant to be me. Forgive me, but do you wish Mr Hartright to remain?

Marion Mr Hartright has seen the letter. He was here when I opened it. Unless *you* would rather he went?

Glyde I've no objection to Mr Hartright's presence. (*He finishes the letter*) Poor demented creature.

Marion You know who wrote it?

Glyde Certainly I do. It's quite apparent to me that this was written by a woman named Anne Catherick. May I ask how it came into your hands?

Marion makes to speak

Hartright (*forestalling her, moving in a little*) I found it lying on the table.

Laura But who is Anne Catherick? What does it all mean?

Glyde It means, my dear, that a very dangerous lunatic is at large. I shall have to inform the authorities.

Laura But why should she be so vindictive about *you*?

Glyde Because she thinks I was the cause of her being restrained.

Laura And were you?

Glyde In a way, yes. (*He sits in the armchair*) Her mother is a tenant of mine at Old Welmington. Quite early in life this girl, her daughter, developed symptoms of a mental affliction which made it necessary for her to be under proper medical care. Mrs Catherick had a natural aversion to allowing her daughter to be placed in a public asylum, so I arranged for her to be admitted to a private home for the insane.

Marion Could Mrs Catherick afford the fees?

Glyde I undertook to be responsible for them.

Laura That was generous of you.

Glyde Unfortunately, the girl discovered my share in having her put away, and conceived an intense hatred of me in consequence. That is all there is to it.

Silence. Glyde looks from one to the other

I can obtain confirmation of everything I say if you wish it.

Marion No, please, that's quite unnecessary.

Glyde (*looking at Laura*) All the same, I think I should prefer it, for my own sake. (*He moves to the desk and scribbles an address*) This is Mrs Catherick's address. Write and ask her whether what I did for her daughter was done with her complete knowledge and sanction. (*He rises and holds the address out to Laura*) It's not ten minutes away. You may have an answer in a quarter of an hour.

Laura No, please. Of course I believe you.

Glyde Then you, Miss Halcombe. (*He moves to Marion*) You need have no
feelings of loyalty towards me.
Marion (*rising and taking the address*) Very well. (*She moves* UL)

Glyde follows Marion

I'll write at once.

Glyde opens the door for her

Remember it is you who wish it.
Glyde I insist upon it.

Marion goes out

(*Moving* C) I'm sorry you've been dragged into this unpleasant affair, Mr
Hartright. Accept my apologies. But the woman is quite insane. (*He
glances at Hartright obliquely*) You caught no glimpse of her, I suppose?
Hartright Why do you ask?
Glyde Naturally, the poor creature must be found as soon as possible for her
own sake. So if you could assist me ——
Hartright I'm sorry. I'm afraid I can't. Will you excuse me? I have to see
Mr Fairlie.

Hartright gives a slight bow, crosses to the door UL *and exits*

Glyde looks after him

Glyde Charming fellow. I must certainly do something for him.
Laura (*too quickly*) Oh, if only you would!

Glyde looks at her

(*Correcting herself*) I mean — he's so clever.
Glyde (*smiling slightly*) So it would appear. (*He sits by her, taking her hand*)
Laura ——
Laura (*rising and moving* L) No, please ... I've something very important
to say to you.
Glyde (*rising*) Oh? (*He waits*) Well?
Laura (*with difficulty*) I want you to — to release me from my engagement
to you.
Glyde (*slowly*) I see. I am to be condemned on the incoherent ravings of a
madwoman.

Laura That has nothing to do with it!

Glyde You must forgive me if I find that difficult to accept.

Laura It's true! (*She moves up to him*) I've said I don't believe the letter! I don't. You've never shown me anything but kindness and affection ——

Glyde (*stiffly*) I'm grateful that my poor endeavours have been noticed.

Laura Please don't make it any harder for me!

Glyde Do you think I find my own position any easier?

Laura (*jerkily*) Please try to understand. When I entered into this engagement I was guided by my father. I thought he knew what was best for me, and I was happy to obey him ——

Glyde But now ——?

Laura Now I realize — it's only fair to tell you — I don't love you. I respect you — I esteem you — but that's all.

Glyde And I value that respect and esteem a hundred times more than the love of any other woman.

Laura Then you'll release me? (*She begins to draw off her engagement ring*)

Glyde No, my dear. (*He moves to her*) I have love enough on my side for both, and I shall hope, in our life together, to win yours. (*He replaces the ring*) Let me put this back.

Laura (*hiding her disappointment*) Then — may I ask you one other thing?

Glyde Of course.

Laura When we return from Italy — would you be angry if Marion came to live with us?

Glyde (*smiling*) Why should I be angry?

Laura Oh, you are kind!

Glyde (*taking Laura's hands*) If the granting of such a little wish can make you happy, then I don't think very much will go wrong with us.

Glyde draws Laura to him. She resists slightly; sensing her slight resistance, Glyde kisses her gently on the forehead

The door opens and Mrs Vesey enters UL

Mrs Vesey Laura dear, be so good as to help me. Mr Fairlie is coming down.

Glyde (*moving away to the fireplace*) At this time of night?

Mrs Vesey (*fetching the screen*) Yes, Sir Percival, and he's so very annoyed. First Mr Hartright came and gave notice, and then Mr Gilmore upset him. (*She places the screen in front of the windows*)

Laura (*startled*) Is Mr Hartright leaving?

Mrs Vesey In the morning, I understand, dear. Mr Fairlie is dreadfully vexed. (*She blows up the fire with the bellows*)

Laura stoops to fetch the footstool from DL *to conceal her dismay. Glyde, who has missed nothing, moves to Laura and takes the footstool from her*

Glyde Allow me. (*He places the stool* C)
Mrs Vesey (*of the fire*) There, I think that will do.

Mr Fairlie's querulous voice floats through the door

Oh, dear, he's here already!
Glyde (*opening the door* UL) This is unexpected, Mr Fairlie.

Mr Fairlie is wheeled in by Louis to C

Mr Fairlie You may well be surprised, Sir Percival. I am far more fit for my bed than for being propelled through draughty corridors. But people delight in annoying me. I noticed it particularly. They combine to plague me. Is that window shut, Mrs Vesey?
Mrs Vesey Yes, Mr Fairlie.
Mr Fairlie Then your skirts are making a draught. Go away.

Mrs Vesey exits UL

I was preparing for a quiet, comfortable night when Mr Hartright, a nonentity whom I'd engaged at a preposterous salary from London, suddenly informs me he must go back to town immediately. No warning — scarcely an apology. Must go, that's all.
Glyde Most irritating. (*He moves to the fireplace*)
Mr Fairlie I tell you, they pick on me. They know I can't retaliate.

Gilmore enters UL. *He stays by the door*

(*Not seeing Gilmore*) I had barely recovered from this, when that horrid Gilmore arrives to tell me there's some hitch in Laura's marriage settlement, and I've got to be adamant about something. As if I could be adamant about anything in my state of health. I ask you, is it likely?
Gilmore (*coming forward*) I hope to persuade you to be, Mr Fairlie.
Mr Fairlie (*quite unperturbed*) Oh, are you there, Gilmore? Come and sit down. Sit down, all of you. I like people to sit down and be quiet and not fidget.

Laura sits on the sofa. Glyde sits DR

Gilmore I prefer to stand.
Mr Fairlie Then kindly keep in one position. Be ready to fan me, Louis. Well, what are we waiting for?
Gilmore For you to stop talking.

Mr Fairlie Oh, how rude you are! You know I haven't the strength to be rude to you back.

Gilmore You manage uncommonly well.

Glyde Do I understand this is something about the marriage settlement, Mr Gilmore?

Gilmore Yes, Sir Percival. As you already know, Miss Fairlie is Mr Fairlie's sole heir, and will inherit his entire property on his death.

Mr Fairlie Which, if I am pestered much more — is likely to occur at any moment.

Gilmore That, however, is straightforward, and needn't trouble us. The point I wish to raise is the disposition of Miss Fairlie's private fortune of eighty thousand pounds ——

Mr Fairlie gives a prodigious yawn

(*Glaring at him*) Mr Fairlie!

Mr Fairlie I beg your pardon, dear Gilmore. Do go on.

Gilmore Now your lawyer, Sir Percival, has made a demand which I consider wholly inadmissible. He insists that, in the event of *your* surviving *her*, Miss Fairlie's fortune should come to you. I, on the other hand, say that she should be at liberty to dispose of it as she pleases. Miss Fairlie, don't you agree with me*?* (*He moves to her*)

Laura (*roused from her thoughts*) I beg your pardon.

Gilmore Wouldn't you prefer to keep this money under your own control? I take it there are some friends or relatives you would like to benefit?

Laura I should like to be able to leave something to Marion. And there is also a — a friend to whom I should like to leave some little remembrance.

Glyde My dear, do you think for one moment I'd oppose you in that?

Gilmore (*moving to Glyde*) That's all very well, Sir Percival, but good intentions are not good in law! I appeal to your sense of justice. Let me arrange for you to have a life interest in the money, and the capital to be disposed of as Miss Fairlie chooses.

Glyde (*rising and moving to the fireplace*) It's useless to appeal to me, Mr Gilmore. I've consented to be guided by my lawyer, and these are the terms he demands.

Gilmore moves back to Mr Fairlie

Mr Fairlie In any case, Gilmore, the whole thing is nonsense! Is it likely, in the first place, that a girl of twenty-one will die before a man of forty-five?

Glyde (*shortly*) Forty.

Mr Fairlie (*sweetly*) Is that all? I beg your pardon. You had some severe illness in your youth, I suppose? In the second place, is a devoted husband the kind of person to prevent his wife from making some little presents to her friends?

Gilmore I don't say it's at all likely in the present circumstances ——
Mr Fairlie Then, pray, what are we all arguing about?
Gilmore But I have known it happen when the circumstances were quite as
favourable as they are now!
Mr Fairlie Poor Gilmore, you must move among some singularly unpleasant
people.
Gilmore (*looking at Mr Fairlie*) I *do*. Mr Fairlie, for the last time I appeal
to you to insist that this clause be altered!
Mr Fairlie Oh, my dear Gilmore, am I well enough to insist upon anything?
Gilmore You refuse?
Mr Fairlie At last we understand each other. I do.
Gilmore Very well. Then I suppose there's no need to delay any further in
signing this. (*He takes a document from his pocket*) I shall need Miss
Halcombe and Mr Hartright as witnesses. (*He rings the bell*)
Mr Fairlie (*plaintively*) Must they come in here?
Gilmore (*going to the desk*) It won't hurt you to breathe the air with six
people for once. (*He brings a pen and the inkstand from the desk to the table
beside the sofa*)
Mr Fairlie You don't know what hurts me, Gilmore, and what's more, you
don't care. My smelling salts, Louis.

Louis hands Mr Fairlie a vial of smelling salts

Mrs Vesey enters UL

Louis pulls Mr Fairlie's chair slightly RC

Gilmore Oh, ask Miss Halcombe and Mr Hartright to step in here, Mrs
Vesey, if you please.
Mrs Vesey Yes, Mr Gilmore.

Mrs Vesey exits

Gilmore I tell you this, Mr Fairlie, with all due respect to Sir Percival Glyde,
that no daughter of mine should be married under such a settlement as
you've sanctioned today! But I wash my hands completely!
Mr Fairlie Oh, dear Gilmore. I wish you would! They smell of horrid
parchments. And I recommend a little eau-de-Cologne in the water. So
refreshing.

Marion and Hartright enter UL

Gilmore Ah, Miss Halcombe, Mr Hartright; I want you both to be witnesses
to Miss Fairlie's signature. (*He spreads out the document on the table*)

Marion What is it?
Gilmore Her marriage settlement.

The eyes of Laura and Hartright meet

Will you sign here, Miss Fairlie?

Laura rises and comes the to table. She signs

Now put your finger on the seal and say, "I deliver this as my act and deed."
Laura I deliver this as my act and deed. (*She sits in the armchair*)
Gilmore Miss Halcombe ——

Marion signs

Now, you, Mr Hartright — below Miss Halcombe's.

Hartright glances at Laura and then signs

Thank you. Well, that's that, and pray heaven it's not a mistake. (*To Laura*)
Goodbye, my dear. God bless you. (*He kisses Laura then moves to Glyde*)
I know you think me a rude old man, Sir Percival, but I hope you'll never
make me regret I didn't stand firm.

Gilmore and Glyde shake hands

Mr Fairlie (*holding out a delicate hand*) Goodbye, dear Gilmore.
Gilmore And as for *you*! (*He seizes Mr Fairlie's hand and wrings it
furiously*)

Gilmore strides out UL

Mr Fairlie (*squealing with pain*) Oh, the ruffian! He's maimed me! To my
room quickly, Louis! My hand is quite crushed! Oh, the barbarian!

Louis wheels Mr Fairlie out UL. *His complaints can be heard along the
corridor*

Marion (*moving* C *and producing a letter*) The reply has come from Mrs
Catherick.

Marion hands the letter to Glyde, who hands it to Laura

Glyde Read it out, my dear.

Laura (*opening the letter and reading*) "In reply to your inquiry, my daughter Anne was placed under medical superintendence with my entire knowledge and approval. The share taken in the matter by Sir Percival Glyde was such as to merit my deepest gratitude towards that gentleman. Your obedient servant, Jane Catherick." What a strange, abrupt letter!
Glyde Mrs Catherick is a strange woman. But it sets your mind at rest?
Laura Completely.

Glyde looks at Marion

Marion Of course.
Glyde Thank you. (*He takes the letter*) Then shall we lay the ghost of Anne Catherick? (*He crushes the letter in his hand and tosses it into the fire*) Now, Mr Hartright, I'm sure you'd like to make your farewells to Miss Halcombe and Miss Fairlie, so I'll leave you. (*He moves to Hartright*) Goodbye and good fortune.

Hartright and Glyde shake hands

(*Moving to the door* UL) I'll be in the study, Laura.

Glyde exits UL

Marion (*moving to Hartright, holding out her hand*) Goodbye, Mr Hartright. I wish it were not necessary for you to go, but I know you are doing right. My best wishes for your future.

Marion and Hartright shake hands

(*Moving to the door* UL) Mr Hartright has something to give you, Laura.

Marion looks from one to the other, then goes out

Hartright (*moving to his drawing*) It's only this. A very trifling wedding gift. But perhaps it may serve as a memento of your home. (*He comes back with it to* C)
Laura (*rising*) Thank you. I shall always value it. (*She hesitates. Desperately*) Mr Hartright, must you really go away?
Hartright I think it's best for me to go … I think it would be wrong if I stayed — much as I wish to.
Laura Yes. (*She holds out her hand*)
Hartright (*taking and holding it*) Miss Fairlie ——
Laura Yes?

Hartright This may sound absurd, but if ever a time should come when you
   feel you need the presence of someone who has your welfare at heart …
   If ever such a time should come — please call on me. Please.
Laura If ever such a time should come, Mr Hartright, I won't hesitate. I
   promise.
Hartright Thank you … Goodbye.

Hartright looks at her once more then goes out quickly

*Laura looks after him, then down at the drawing. She presses it to her lips
as* ——

—— *the* CURTAIN *falls*

ACT II
SCENE 1

The same. November 1861

Hartright's drawing of Old Welmington Church hangs over the fireplace. The furniture has been slightly re-arranged, and the sofa is now placed C, *facing the audience, a small table set in front of it. The armchair* R *is now a little further* DS, *so that anyone sitting in it may address anyone sitting on the sofa easily. (If preferred, the screen, footstool and footwarmer may be removed)*

The CURTAIN *rises. Marion enters* UL *carrying a tray of tea things including a plate of small cakes. Mrs Vesey follows, wearing outdoor clothes, and carrying a bag*

Marion (*as she enters*) I'll take these, Mrs Vesey. You shall bring in the tea when they arrive. (*She puts the tray on the table before the sofa*)

Mrs Vesey Marion, do you think I should? I have no place here any more.

Marion But you shall have a new place very soon. Laura will be delighted to have you as her housekeeper when she and Sir Percival go to Blackwater Park.

Mrs Vesey But if Mr Fairlie knew I was still here ——

Marion Well, he won't. He's safe enough in his hydro for a month, thinking about his imaginary complaints.

Mrs Vesey Well, if you say so, Marion. But I have my bag packed if dear Laura shouldn't want me. (*She places her bag by the door* UL)

Marion She will, so stop worrying. What time is it? (*She moves to the fireplace and looks at the clock*) Almost four. They'll be here any moment now.

Mrs Vesey (*taking off her bonnet and mantle and placing them on the chair* DL) How pleasant it will be for you to have dear Laura home again.

Marion Yes, indeed. I've missed her.

Mrs Vesey But you won't be parted again. You'll be going to live with them at Blackwater Park when the house is ready.

Marion I hope so.

Mrs Vesey Hope so? But I thought it was all arranged.

Marion I thought so, too, but … Mrs Vesey, did Laura write to you from Italy? (*She moves to the sofa*)

Mrs Vesey Yes, dear, several times. Such delightful letters they were, too. Surely you heard from her as well, Marion? (*She moves to the sofa*)

Marion Yes, of course, but — (*she sits on the sofa*) Mrs Vesey, didn't it strike you there was something very strange about her letters?

Mrs Vesey Strange? Whatever do you mean, dear?

Marion Didn't you notice she wrote only about the places they'd been to — the art galleries and museums and so on? Nothing at all about herself or her husband — or even his greatest friend Count Fosco.

Mrs Vesey You forget, Marion, it must have been such a novelty for her, travelling to all those places.

Marion Yes, I suppose so. But I should have thought that on one's honeymoon one writes to say one is happy.

Mrs Vesey Oh, my dear, you're being fanciful!

Marion Perhaps I am. (*She rises and moves to the fireplace*) Do you think Mr Hartright's drawing of Old Welmington Church looks well there? I hope Laura will like the frame I've chosen.

Mrs Vesey You've placed it beautifully, dear, and it was a charming thought to have it framed for her.

Marion I thought she would like it.

Mrs Vesey What a pleasant young man Mr Hartright was.

Marion Yes, indeed. (*She listens*) Is that the carriage? (*She runs to the window*) Yes, it is! She's here. Mrs Vesey! Laura's here! (*She heads for the door* UL)

Mrs Vesey (*moving to the window and looking out*) Don't go and meet her, dear.

Marion Not meet Laura!

Mrs Vesey There are strangers with them. They're just getting out of the carriage.

Marion Yes, I forgot. (*She returns and looks out of the window*) They must be Count and Countess Fosco. Oh, Mrs Vesey, to see Laura again after all these months!

Laura enters UL. *She looks unhappy*

(*Moving to Laura*) Laura!

Laura Marion! Oh, Marion dear, how lovely to see you!

Marion Welcome home, Laura darling.

They embrace

Mrs Vesey My dear Laura.

Laura (*breaking away and moving to Mrs Vesey*) Mrs Vesey! Did you stay to welcome me? Oh, how kind! (*She kisses Mrs Vesey*) My uncle wrote that you were leaving here.

Marion She is, Laura. Uncle Frederick has told her to go, after all her years of service.

Mrs Vesey No, Marion dear, that isn't quite correct.

Marion As nearly as makes no matter.

Mrs Vesey (*to Laura*) He explained to me that now you were both going away, he preferred a bachelor establishment — and I daresay it's true I am a little past my work.

Laura Did he say that? Oh, how monstrous of him!

Marion But you'll help her, Laura, won't you?

Laura Help her?

Marion When you go to Blackwater Park. You'll need a housekeeper. Sir Percival can have no objection ——

Laura turns away

Laura, don't say you don't want her either!

Laura No — no, it's not that — only — (*with difficulty*) my husband wishes us to live very simply ——

Marion But it's for you to say what staff's to be engaged!

Laura You don't understand, Marion. But I'll do what I can, Mrs Vesey. I'll ask him if you may come with us.

Mrs Vesey Thank you, dear. (*She moves to the door* UL) I'll bring in the tea now. I'm sure you must need it after your journey.

Mrs Vesey exits UL

Marion Laura, have you been ill? You look different. So much paler.

Laura (*taking off her hat and putting it on the chair* DR) No. The heat of Italy didn't agree with me, that's all. I shall be better now I'm back in England and have you beside me. (*She suddenly turns to Marion*) You *will* stay with me, won't you, Marion?

Marion Of course I will. I said I would.

Laura (*desperately*) But you must promise me! Promise!

Marion (*astonished*) Laura, what's wrong?

Laura (*moving away*) Nothing.

Marion (*following*) That's not true! Something's badly wrong! Won't you tell me what it is? You know you can trust me.

Laura Ssh! He may be listening! (*She gives a terrified glance at the door* UL)

Marion Your husband?

Laura No, Count Fosco.

Marion looks at Laura, then makes to go to the door UL

No, don't do that! (*She draws Marion back*) You don't know him. I think he watches me all the time. Both of them do! (*She brings Marion* DR)

Marion Both?

Laura He and his dreadful wife who hardly ever speaks. (*She covers her face*) Oh, Marion!

Marion Laura, you're distraught! Why should the Count watch you?

Laura I don't know. I only know that when you think yourself quite alone, he's suddenly at your elbow. He terrifies me!

Marion Laura ——

The door UL *opens*

Laura (*seeing this*) Sssh!

Laura grasps Marion's hand, and they wait, rigid and silent

> *The door opens fully, and Count Fosco, a stout, bland, smiling man of middle age, enters. He is dressed in indoor clothes. Although his manner is bland and genial, there is nonetheless a sinister air about him, and he watches Laura constantly*

Fosco Ah, my dear ladies, you are here. I come to make myself known. This is the famous Miss Halcombe, I doubt not. (*He offers his hand*)

Laura (*trembling*) Marion — this is Count Fosco.

Marion (*taking the offered hand*) Famous is scarcely the word, I'm afraid, Count.

Fosco No? But famous in your language means well-known, does it not? And I know you well.

Marion How could you?

Fosco (*smiling*) Because Lady Glyde here, she never cease speaking of Marion, the kind half-sister. If my friend Glyde were not so good a man, he might well be jealous of the place you hold in his Laura's heart.

Laura sits on the sofa. Marion sits by her. Fosco moves to the chair DL

> Well, and what do you think of your sister, Miss Halcombe? Does she look well after her sojourn in my beautiful country? (*He sits*)

Marion Not as well as I had hoped.

Fosco Ah, we could not give her all the comfort we had wished. But next time she come to Italy, if God be good, it shall be to the Villa Fosco.

> *Countess Fosco glides in* UL. *She is a tight-lipped, tight-curled figure, silent and watchful. She carries a little box from the contents of which she perpetually rolls cigarettes for the Count. She has discarded her outdoor things*

(*Rising and moving up to Countess Fosco*) Ah, Eleanor, my love, you must meet Miss Halcombe. My sweet wife, the Countess. (*He brings her* DL)

Countess Fosco bows frigidly, then sits DL *and rolls a cigarette*

I have been telling Miss Halcombe of our hope one day to repossess the Villa Fosco.
Marion Has it passed from your family, Count?
Fosco Alas, yes. But soon we shall have the means to buy it back again.

Laura rises and goes towards the door UL. *Fosco immediately steps in front of her. Countess Fosco rises*

You wish something, Lady Glyde?
Laura (*nervously*) I was wondering why tea was so late.
Fosco Permit me to ring the bell. (*He does so and moves* DL *again*)

Countess Fosco hands Fosco a cigarette, then sits

Thank you, my angel. (*He kisses the tips of her fingers*) Is she not a treasure, Miss Halcombe? She knows to the minute when this unhealthy craving comes upon me.

Mrs Vesey enters UL *with the teapot*

Laura (*sitting on the sofa*) Thank you, Mrs Vesey. Put it here by me.

Mrs Vesey puts the teapot on the table by Laura

Tea, Countess?

Countess Fosco inclines her head. Laura pours out

Fosco Ah, plenty of sweet cakes. That is good.
Laura (*handing a cup to Mrs Vesey*) For the Countess.

Mrs Vesey takes the cup of tea to Countess Fosco

Fosco (*taking the cake plate*) Let me give you a cake, Miss Halcombe.
Marion No, thank you.
Fosco No? Then, Eleanor, my dear? Lady Glyde?

All refuse

No? Well, the more for Fosco. He has what you call the sweet tooth. (*He sits in the armchair* R)

Mrs Vesey hands him tea

Ah, thank you — thank you.
Glyde (*off*) What the devil ——?

Glyde enters UL. *He has shed his suave and courteous manner of the first Act, and is at present in a very bad temper*

Mrs Vesey is momentarily out of his view

Must that infernal luggage be left in the hall? Get somebody to move it!

Laura rises, but Fosco makes a sign to his wife

Fosco My angel.

Countess Fosco glides out silently

Laura sits. Glyde moves to the sideboard, his back to the room

Marion (*rising*) How are you, Sir Percival? (*She moves to him*)
Glyde None the better for being kept out of my house for three months. To say nothing of this confounded journey to Cumberland.
Laura Marion will help us get your house in order — won't you, Marion? (*She pours a cup of tea and holds it out to Mrs Vesey*)

Mrs Vesey approaches and takes the cup of tea

Glyde What's Miss Halcombe to do with it?
Laura She's coming to live with us. Don't you remember? I asked you and you said she might.
Glyde (*to Marion*) And you're all packed and ready, I suppose? I'm to be the provider in the future, am I? Just as a change from Fairlie!

Marion draws back. Mrs Vesey approaches Glyde timidly with the cup of tea

Mrs Vesey Sir Percival ——

Glyde turns and sees Mrs Vesey

Glyde (*staring*) What the devil are you doing here? Fairlie wrote to me you'd been discharged.

Mrs Vesey I have, Sir Percival, but Marion said ——
Marion Poor Mrs Vesey had no place to go. I thought that you and
Laura ——
Glyde (*moving to the sofa*) Might take her to live with us as well, eh? My
God, that's cool! (*To Laura*) First one and then the other of your broken-
down pensioners!
Laura (*rising*) Marion's not a pensioner!
Glyde Indeed? Will she be paying for her board and lodging? We're not
wealthy, you know, Miss Halcombe. At least, I'm not. (*He moves back to
the sideboard*) My dear wife — as she is never tired of reminding me —
has all the money! (*He picks up the decanter, finds it empty, and sets it down
with an exclamation of annoyance*) Fosco, I left some bottles of wine in the
other room. Come and help me fetch them. (*He moves towards the door* UL)
Fosco (*rising*) If you will pardon me, ladies.
Glyde Oh, come on! (*He sees Mrs Vesey's bag by the door*) Whose bag is
this?
Mrs Vesey Mine, Sir Percival.
Glyde Is it? Then kindly take it out of this room!

*Glyde exits followed by Fosco. Mrs Vesey picks up her bag and exits after
them*

Laura sits on the sofa

Laura I'm sorry, Marion! I'm so sorry!
Marion What's happened, Laura? What's changed him? (*She sits by Laura*)
Laura I believe he is very worried ——
Marion Don't make excuses for him! Has he been like this ever since you
married him?
Laura Yes. From the very first day.
Marion But I don't understand. He loved you.
Laura No, Marion, don't deceive yourself. He never loved me — never for
one moment. And I'm bound to him for the rest of my life! Oh, Marion,
please stay with me if you can bear it. But if you'd rather not, I won't blame
you.
Marion I promised I'd stay, and I meant it. But can you tell me one thing?
What has Count Fosco to do with all this?
Laura I believe he has some hold over my husband ——
Marion Hold?
Laura I think Sir Percival is afraid of him. But why, I don't know.

Mrs Vesey enters UL. *She carries a letter*

Yes, Mrs Vesey, what is it?

Mrs Vesey (*handing the letter to Laura*) This letter has just come for Sir Percival, dear.
Laura Thank you, I'll give it to him.

Glyde and Fosco enter at that moment, carrying bottles of wine

Glyde All right, I'll take it. (*To Mrs Vesey*) Decant this, if you know how.

Glyde hands Mrs Vesey two bottles and takes the letter from Laura

Mrs Vesey exits with the bottles and decanter

Fosco places his bottles on the sideboard

Fosco (*looking at Laura and Marion sitting together*) I fear we are interrupting a charming reunion, my friend.
Glyde (*uncorking a bottle*) Bosh! Laura's only been whining to Miss Halcombe of how badly I treat her. Isn't that so, Miss Halcombe?
Marion (*rising*) I'll help you unpack, Laura.

Laura rises. She and Marion move UL

Glyde I shall want you here in ten minutes. *You*, Laura — not your shadow.
Marion (*at the door*) Was it necessary for you to shed all your manners after your courtship, Sir Percival?

Laura and Marion go out UL

Fosco (*savagely*) Sometimes I think you are the biggest fool alive!
Glyde (*pouring himself a glass of wine*) Oh, don't preach!
Fosco Must you antagonize them both? I can see at a glance — I, Fosco, who have not been in this house half an hour — that your wife will be advised by Miss Halcombe. Win over the sister, and you win them both!
Glyde I'm sick of wheedling! Do you know how long I smiled and smirked for that whey-faced doll? First with her father and then with her. Eight years. Eight years! And for what? To marry the dullest woman in England! (*He drinks*)
Fosco *And* to marry eighty thousand pounds — of which you owe me ten.
Glyde I owe you five!
Fosco You owe me ten! When I lent you that five thousand for your courtship, you promised me double in return — that I might buy back the Villa Fosco — my ancestral home.
Glyde What good would that be to you? You can never live there. You've a pleasant little record, Fosco, of spying against your own country!

Fosco That will not be known. (*He moves close to Glyde*) And you will never tell it, my friend, for fear that I should break you in return.

Glyde (*terrified*) Hold your tongue!

Fosco Precisely. (*He sits on the sofa*) We will not ruin each other. Though I am not such a fool as to have placed the power of ruining me into more than one hand. Has the woman Anne Catherick been traced yet?

Glyde (*moving to the sideboard and refilling his glass*) No. I've spent more than I dare think of trying to trace her and she eludes my people every time. (*He drinks*)

Fosco Open your letter while you're still sober enough to read it.

Glyde (*handing Fosco the letter*) I don't need to read it. I know what it contains.

Fosco (*opening the letter*) So — your creditors are giving you one month to settle?

Glyde One day will be enough. I have the papers ready. I shall make Laura sign this now (*he takes out a document*) and post it to my lawyer tonight. (*He pulls the bell-cord*)

Fosco (*rising*) And how do you propose to make her sign?

Glyde She's my wife, isn't she?

Fosco That, she must be painfully aware of.

Glyde Then she'll do what I tell her to!

Mrs Vesey enters

Tell Lady Glyde to come here at once.

Mrs Vesey looks astonished

Fosco (*smoothly*) Ask Lady Glyde to be so good as to come here.

Mrs Vesey Yes, sir.

Mrs Vesey exits UL

Fosco We still have to face the possibility of her refusal. (*He puts the letter on the mantelpiece*)

Glyde You don't think I'm going to let her know what's in this, do you? (*He taps the document*) Besides, she won't refuse. She knows what to expect if she crosses me.

Fosco I still say treat her gently. Remember she is no longer alone.

Glyde What could her sister do?

Fosco Much.

Glyde Rubbish!

Fosco She is a woman of strength and courage. I say again, be careful!

Laura enters UL

Laura (*quietly*) You asked for me?
Glyde Yes.
Fosco (*moving to her; quickly*) Your husband wishes to speak to you, Lady Glyde. Please sit down.

Fosco brings Laura to the armchair RC

(*To Glyde*) Do you wish me to remain?
Glyde Do as you please.
Fosco Then I will go and smoke a cigarette in the garden. (*He heads for the french windows. To Glyde, low, as he passes him*) For my sake, if not for your own, be sensible.

Fosco exits through the french windows

Glyde, at the sideboard, makes to pour another drink, then changes his mind. He moves to Laura, resuming his former gentle and courteous manner

Glyde Laura ——
Laura Well?
Glyde I owe you an apology, Laura.
Laura For what, in particular?
Glyde For making you unhappy these past few weeks.
Laura I've wished myself dead. I know now you never loved me, but why did you marry me? Why?
Glyde You're wrong, Laura. I do love you. I always have. It's you who has never had the slightest affection for me. Why didn't you tell me there was someone else?
Laura You — *know*?
Glyde (*nodding*) Why didn't you tell me?
Laura It was so hopeless ... I was pledged to you. I *did* ask you to release me ——
Glyde But I didn't know then. Was it fair, Laura, to give me second best?
Laura (*rising*) I meant to be a good wife to you! I *have* tried!
Glyde (*walking to the mantelpiece, and touching the drawing*) With your mind on *him* all the time. (*He turns and faces her*) That first night after our marriage, when we crossed on the Channel Packet. I had such plans for us. I'd won you at last. I meant to win your love as well. Then *his* name was mentioned casually by another passenger, and your attention was gone from me. I might never have existed. I knew in that moment that I'd attained — with all my efforts — a wife with more affection for him in her little finger than she had for me in her whole body.

Laura You make me feel ashamed ... I didn't understand ... I didn't know I'd hurt you. (*She sits on the sofa*)

Glyde I behaved badly to you after that, I know, but all my hopes — all my plans had come crashing down.

Laura What do you mean?

Glyde When one is loved it's easy to ask favours; it's impossible when one is not.

Laura Had you a favour to ask of me? Tell me what it is?

Glyde Laura, I can't.

Laura Please. I've made you unhappy enough. We'll put the past behind us — we'll begin again — if only you'll help me and be kind to me ——

Glyde (*sitting by Laura and taking her hands*) Laura.

Laura Tell me what I can do. Is it money you need?

He is silent

Is it?

Glyde Yes. I never concealed from Mr Fairlie that I wasn't wealthy.

Laura I know that.

Glyde My father left the estate in bad shape, and for years I've been trying to pull it round. Now I need a small sum to put some of the farms in order.

Laura I'll write at once to Mr Gilmore —— (*She rises*)

Glyde (*quickly*) That won't be necessary. (*He rises*)

Laura But surely he must ——

Glyde (*producing the document and going to the desk*) My solicitor has drawn this up. It makes over to me from your estate the amount I need. You've only to sign it. (*He folds the paper down half-way and puts a paperweight on the folded half*) That is, if you will.

Laura Of course I will. Most willingly.

Glyde (*lifting Laura's hand to his lips*) I'll call Fosco and Miss Halcombe to witness your signature.

Laura sits at the desk and prepares to sign

(*Moving to the french windows. Calling*) Fosco!

Glyde exits UL

(*Off*) Miss Halcombe!

Laura reaches for a pen and in doing so knocks the paperweight aside. The paper springs back and reveals the rest of the writing. She is about to replace the weight when her attention is riveted by the contents of the document. She picks it up and begins to read

Glyde enters, sees what Laura is doing and starts towards her

Laura rises and moves away from Glyde DR, *holding the paper*

Put that down!

Fosco enters through the french windows

Laura So your small sum to repair the farms was eighty thousand pounds!
Glyde I couldn't tell you all I owed! I hated to deceive you ——
Laura Oh, don't lie to me any more!
Glyde Laura!
Laura I've been foolish, but don't treat me like a child! Why have you tried to rob me?
Fosco Rob is a very harsh word, Lady Glyde.

Marion enters UL

Laura What other word is there for it? (*Moving to Marion*) Read this, Marion! Sir Percival wished me to sign it without seeing the contents!
Marion It's everything you have!
Laura Yes — everything I have. (*To Glyde*) Why do you want this money?
Glyde I'm not bound to explain to you!
Laura Nor am I bound to help you!
Glyde You're my wife — it's your duty to do as I say! You'll sign this paper or I won't answer for the consequences!
Fosco (*moving down to Glyde*) Control your temper, you fool!
Glyde (*shaking Fosco off*) Leave me alone! (*Moving to Laura*) I'll give you twenty-four hours to think it over. At the end of that time I advise you to be ready to sign!

Glyde exits R

Fosco You must not heed him, Lady Glyde. He has an unfortunate temper and has been much worried of late. I will speak to him.

Fosco follows Glyde out

Marion Laura, what does it mean?
Laura (*sitting on the sofa*) It means this is what he married me for. I stood up to him this time, but I may not always be able to do so. He has ways — you don't know … Oh, Marion, what am I going to do?
Marion (*sitting by Laura*) Don't, my love … don't cry. We'll find a way out. I'll write to Mr Gilmore. He will advise us what to do.

Laura But it will take two days to get an answer — and he may try again!

Marion I'll ask for a reply by special messenger. Then we shall hear by tomorrow. Be of good courage, my love.

Laura Oh, Marion, what would I do without you?

Marion (*kissing Laura*) Go to your room now. If Sir Percival comes, say you're resting. Don't see him again today.

They rise

Laura And you'll write at once?

Marion At once. I promise.

Marion takes Laura to the door UL

  Laura exits

Marion goes to the desk, and after a moment's thought begins to write

  Mrs Vesey enters UL

(*Jumping*) Oh, Mrs Vesey, how you startled me!

Mrs Vesey I came for my bonnet and mantle, dear. There's a train at six o'clock. I hope to catch it.

Marion No — you mustn't go, Mrs Vesey!

Mrs Vesey My dear, I must. I can't stay after what Sir Percival said.

Marion I want you to stay — just a few days longer. Please, Mrs Vesey — Laura needs every friend she has.

Mrs Vesey I see that, Marion, only too plainly.

Marion And I need you, too. (*As she writes*) I'm writing to Mr Gilmore, and his reply will come by special messenger ——

Mrs Vesey But, Marion, I still don't understand why ——

Marion I must stay with Laura every moment that I can, so I shall want you, Mrs Vesey, to fetch the letter for me. (*She folds the letter and seals it*)

Mrs Vesey (*moving to* L *of desk*) What has happened, Marion?

Marion I can't tell you all, but I fear it will be impossible for Laura to stay here. (*She rises*) Go and put your things away now, there's a dear. I must put this letter in the postbag before it's taken to the village.

Marion exits UL

Mrs Vesey moves DL *and takes up her bonnet and mantle*

  Fosco enters R

Fosco Ah, the good Mrs Vesey! The very person I wished to see. I had no chance to make myself known before. I am Count Fosco.

Mrs Vesey (*curtsying*) Good-afternoon, Count.

Fosco (*at his most affable*) I have heard so much about you, Mrs Vesey. You have been here for a very long time, I believe? (*He sits on the arm of the sofa*)

Mrs Vesey Yes, sir, I have. For thirty years.

Fosco Thirty years. It *is* a long time. You have seen Lady Glyde grow up then from a child?

Mrs Vesey Oh, yes, indeed, sir. I think, sometimes, after poor Mrs Fairlie died, she almost looked upon me as a mother.

Fosco I'm sure she did. I am so sorry for her.

Mrs Vesey For Lady Glyde? You, sir?

Fosco Oh, I know you think I am the friend of her husband — and so it is. I am. But I am shamed to see the way he treats her. Poor Lady Glyde. She needs some good advice.

Mrs Vesey Oh, but Miss Halcombe has already advised her, sir.

Fosco Indeed?

Mrs Vesey Only this very moment she's written to Mr Gilmore in London.

Fosco (*smiling*) I am so glad.

Mrs Vesey Oh, sir, what a joy it is to discover you are her friend as well!

Fosco (*rising*) Ah, but I must beg you do not speak of it to either of the ladies. You realize I must affect to keep on good terms with Sir Percival.

Mrs Vesey Oh, I do, sir.

Fosco But you may tell me everything they do in perfect confidence, and I will do all that is in my power to assist. (*He pats her hand*)

Mrs Vesey Oh, God bless you, sir! You've taken such a weight off my mind!

Fosco That is what I wished. Go along now, Mrs Vesey.

Mrs Vesey exits UL

Fosco chuckles, moves to the desk, picks up the blotting paper and holds it to the mirror. He purses his lips as though soundlessly whistling at what he sees. Then he listens, replaces the blotting paper quickly, and exits L

Marion enters UL. *She tears the blotting paper to pieces and throws it in the fire. Then she opens her reticule, takes out a notecase and counts the money she has in it*

Anne Catherick appears at the french windows and taps gently on them. She is dressed entirely in white, including a white fringed shawl

Marion does not hear. The tap is repeated. Marion turns, stifles a gasp at seeing someone at the window. Anne beckons her. She goes slowly to the windows, then, thinking she recognizes Laura, opens them quickly

Marion Laura — what are you doing out there? (*She backs away* R) You're not Laura!

Anne (*staying by the windows*) I'm Anne Catherick. I must see Miss Fairlie! Please, I *must* see her!

Marion Miss Fairlie is not well enough to see anyone.

Anne Please! I have risked so much to see her. Are you her friend?

Marion I am her sister.

Anne Then let me speak to you! It is very, very important.

Marion Wait! (*She crosses and locks the doors,* UL; *then goes to the door* R) There's no key to this. (*She places a chair under the handle*) Now, come in.

Anne enters the room

It's uncanny— your likeness to my sister.

Anne clings to a chair

Sit down. You're tired.

Anne No— I'm not tired ... I am very ill ... (*She sits in the armchair* R) What is your name? (*During the following, she picks at her white shawl with her nervous fingers and pulls off and drops, unnoticed, a piece of the white fringe*)

Marion Marion Halcombe.

Anne I must say to you what I had hoped to say to your sister, Miss Halcombe, because — I am dying.

Marion Oh, no! You're ill, as you say, but —— (*She kneels by Anne*)

Anne It is true, Miss Halcombe, and I must make atonement.

Marion Atonement? For what? You've done us no injury.

Anne I have done Miss Fairlie a great injury. I could have prevented her disastrous marriage, but I was afraid to speak out. I couldn't help it, Miss Halcombe! Wouldn't you be afraid of a man who shut you up in a madhouse, and would do so again if he could?

Marion But you are no longer afraid?

Anne No. If they catch me now — I wouldn't be there very long.

Marion makes a sympathetic movement

Don't pity me, Miss Halcombe. I shall be happy to join dear Mrs Fairlie.

Marion (*with a glance at the door*) I don't wish to hurry you, but we must be quick.

Anne (*passing a hand over her forehead*) What was I saying? When Mrs Fairlie is in my mind, all else goes from it.

Marion You were saying you could have prevented my sister's marriage ——

Anne Yes, yes, that was it. It's too late for that now, but I can give her a weapon to fight him with. He has a secret, Miss Halcombe ——

Marion Secret?

Anne A secret he is terrified of anybody knowing! I threatened him with it once — that's why he put me in the madhouse! But if Miss Fairlie knew it, then he wouldn't dare to treat her badly!

Marion How did you learn of it?

Anne I heard him and my mother speak of it once when they didn't know I was by. He gives my mother money to keep it ——

The handle of the door R is turned. Marion sees it turn and grips Anne's arm. The door is tapped

Marion Yes? Who is it?

Fosco (*off*) I, Fosco.

Marion The door is locked. I have a headache. I'm trying to rest.

Fosco (*off*) Your pardon, Miss Halcombe. I will not disturb you.

Marion (*softly*) We mustn't go on talking. He may have heard your voice. You must come back tomorrow. When can you come?

Anne I don't know. But I will leave a message for you.

Marion Where?

Anne At the grave of dear Mrs Fairlie. I'll write a note and leave it in a bunch of flowers.

Marion Very well.

Anne You promise you'll tell Miss Fairlie what I've said?

Marion (*rising*) Every word. But you shall see her yourself tomorrow. Yes, and Mr Gilmore!

Anne Who is he? (*She rises*)

Marion Her friend and lawyer. I've written to him tonight. Now I shall add a postscript to my letter, telling him to come here himself. You shall speak in front of *him*! Now, go quickly!

Anne Thank you for listening to me, Miss Halcombe — and for not thinking me mad.

Anne slips out through the french windows

Marion shuts the windows after Anne, removes the chair from the door R, unlocks the door UL, exits and returns almost immediately with her letter. She breaks the seal, sits at the desk and writes quickly, adding more to the letter

Fosco enters R

Fosco Ah, you are rested, Miss Halcombe?
Marion Yes, thank you. I wished to add a few lines to my letter.

While her back is still turned, Fosco notices the piece of white fringe torn from Anne Catherick's shawl, on the floor. He looks at it, smiling, then slips it into his pocket. Marion reseals her letter and rises

Fosco I hope your letter is not important, Miss Halcombe.
Marion It is. Very important. It must go tonight.

Countess Fosco enters quietly. She stands before the doors UL *and nods to Fosco*

Fosco That is unfortunate.
Marion Unfortunate?
Fosco The postbag has just gone to the village.
Marion Gone? But it was there a moment ago!
Fosco True. But now it has just gone. Your letter will not go tonight, Miss Halcombe … Such a pity!

Marion, between the Foscos, looks from one to the other. They look back at her, unmoving, Fosco smiling, his wife expressionless, as ——

—— *the* CURTAIN *falls*

SCENE 2

The same. Two days later. Late evening

The furniture is arranged as in ACT I. *The screen, footstool and footwarmer are again in their original positions. Coffee is set on the sofa table and there is a bowl of flowers on the table* L *and some embroidery on the arm of the sofa*

When the CURTAIN *rises, the lamps are lighted and the french windows are open*

Laura stands by the door R, *pressed against it, listening*

Marion appears at the windows, a shawl about her shoulders. She holds a note

Laura Marion ——
Marion (*entering*) Is it safe to talk?
Laura Yes, they're still in the dining-room. Did you see Anne Catherick?
Marion No, she wasn't there. But she left this note as she promised. Read it quickly.
Laura (*taking the note from Marion. Reading*) "I was ill yesterday and could not come. I must see you tonight for I am told I have only a few days to live." Marion!
Marion Quickly!
Laura (*reading*) "I shall wait outside your house. When it is safe for me to come in, place a bowl of flowers in the window, and we will speak again of your husband's secret. Don't fail me. I shall never again be able to help you."
Marion Laura, *you* must see her tonight. It may be your last chance to free yourself.
Laura But what does it matter what she tells us? We've no means of using her information. There's been no reply to your letter to Mr Gilmore.
Marion No. Either my own letter or the reply has been intercepted … Laura, I'm going to London tonight to see him.
Laura Mr Gilmore?
Marion Yes. There's a train at ten o'clock. I shall go straight to his private house and bring him back with me tomorrow.
Laura (*moving to Marion*) But you'll never get away from here! You know how they watch us!
Marion Yes, but by the mercy of providence Sir Percival is away until tomorrow. That leaves only Fosco and his wife ——
Laura But ——
Marion Listen. As soon as they come in here I shall say I'm going to bed. I've a bag concealed in the hall. I shall slip straight out of the house and run for the station. They can't pursue me. Sir Percival has taken the only horses in the stable.
Laura But, Marion, don't you see ——?
Marion What?
Laura (*sitting on the sofa*) I shall be alone with — Fosco.
Marion Don't be afraid, my love. He'll do nothing to you. He's only a guard on us, and I shall be back tomorrow. Wait in your room till all is quiet, then come down and place this bowl of flowers in the window. (*She indicates the bowl on the table* L)
Laura How shall I know Anne Catherick?
Marion (*moving back to the table where the coffee is set*) Very easily.
Laura How?
Marion (*sitting on the sofa*) I haven't told you this before — but she is the exact counterpart of yourself.

Laura Of *me*?

Marion You might be her twin — except that she looks so pale and ill — as I'm afraid you're doing.

Laura How strange — to resemble me so much ... I wish we could do something for her.

Marion If what the poor creature says is true, there's nothing anyone can do. But I have a feeling, Laura, that she'll bring you your release.

Laura presses Marion's hand

Now let us have our coffee and look as composed as we can.

Laura I wish you weren't leaving me, Marion.

Marion I wish I weren't. But it's our only chance.

The door R opens. Marion sees it opening and changes her tone

That's exquisite embroidery, Laura. I wish I were as clever. (*She hands the embroidery to Laura*)

Fosco enters R

Marion Ah, Count Fosco, you're late for your coffee.

Fosco Your pardon, Miss Halcombe — Lady Glyde.

Laura (*pouring coffee*) Where is the Countess?

Fosco My indefatigable angel is rolling me some more cigarettes in the dining-room. I have been greedy with them tonight.

Laura hands Fosco a cup of coffee

Ah, thank you. This is cosy, is it not? It is not friendly to say so perhaps, but how pleasant it is when Sir Percival is away. (*He sits in the armchair*)

Laura Where did he go, Count?

Fosco To visit one of his farms. A tenant is fractious, he says, but I fear it is Glyde who is difficult.

Marion (*rising*) I'll say good-night, Laura.

A look passes between Laura and Marion

Fosco (*rising*) So soon? It is barely half-past nine.

Marion Yes, but we were late last night, if you remember.

Fosco True, and you wish to obtain the sleep of beauty? Perhaps you think it would be well if Fosco took some? (*He chuckles and puts his cup on the sideboard*)

Marion (*smiling*) One cannot improve upon perfection, Count.
Fosco Ah, how kind!

Fosco kisses Marion's hand, then moves UL *to the door*

Marion Good-night, Laura. (*She kisses Laura*) Good-night, Count. (*She moves* UL)
Fosco Good-night. (*He opens the door for her*) Sleep well, Miss Halcombe.

Marion exits UL

Fosco (*looking after her*) Charming — charming!
Laura Count Fosco ——
Fosco (*moving to the armchair*) Lady Glyde?
Laura I would like to ask you something.
Fosco I am all attention. (*He sits*)
Laura Do you think if I offered Sir Percival money he would let me go?
Fosco My dear lady!
Laura Oh, don't pretend to be shocked! You must know as well as anyone that he married me for one thing only — my money!
Fosco Perhaps.
Laura Would he, do you think? Please, Count, tell me!
Fosco It is impossible for me to say. He is in great difficulties, you know ——
Laura So I believe.
Fosco It would depend, no doubt, upon the amount of moneys.
Laura Ten thousand pounds?
Fosco It is a fair sum ——
Laura Then will you tell him?
Fosco I will tell him, but I fear … (*He spreads his hands*)
Laura But he doesn't love me. Money is all he wants.
Fosco I will speak to him. (*He rises and moves to the sideboard*) And now the game of cards, yes?
Laura (*rising*) Not tonight, Count. I have some orders to give to Mrs Vesey. Then I shall go up to bed.
Fosco Fosco is deserted tonight. But you do not look well, Lady Glyde, so I shall not attempt to dissuade you. (*He opens the door* UL) Until tomorrow.
Laura Good-night.

Laura exits UL

Fosco smiles, closes the door, takes the piece of white fringe from his pocket and looks at it

Countess Fosco enters through the french windows carrying a note

Fosco Well?

Countess Fosco (*handing Fosco the note*) Hidden where you heard her say. I copied it and then replaced it. (*She closes the french windows and the curtains*)

Fosco Did Miss Halcombe come?

Countess Fosco Yes. She read it, then hurried back to the house.

Fosco (*glancing through the note*) Tonight! So Anne Catherick comes tonight. (*Reading*) "When it is safe, place a bowl of flowers in the window ——"

Countess Fosco Listen! (*She moves towards the UL door*)

Fosco (*moving to her, stopping her*) It is only Miss Halcombe leaving for the station. She thinks she has outwitted us, my angel. She does not guess that Fosco intercepted her letter so she would be forced to leave her darling Laura alone. She thinks it is by accident that Glyde is out of the house so that her escape is made easy ——

Glyde enters R

What are you doing here? (*He moves to Glyde*) You are half an hour before your time!

Glyde I'm lucky to be here at all! My gig broke down a mile away. (*He moves to the sideboard and pours himself a drink from the decanter*) Now perhaps you'll be good enough to tell me why I've been kept away from the house in this fashion!

Fosco Speak low. Your wife may be within hearing.

Glyde Where's Miss Halcombe?

Fosco Gone to catch the London train.

Glyde Gone! (*He moves to Fosco*) You blundering fool! Don't you know she'll go straight to Gilmore?

Fosco Control yourself! I wished for her to go!

Glyde You wished ... ! Are you trying to ruin me?

Countess Fosco moves to the chair DL and sits

Fosco No, my friend. I am trying to save you. Listen, and use what little brain you have! What is the most important thing to you at this moment?

Glyde The capture of Anne Catherick, I suppose.

Fosco Exactly. The capture of Anne Catherick. Now attend to me. Two days ago Miss Halcombe had a secret visitor ——

Glyde (*terrified*) Not ——

Fosco Yes, my friend. Anne Catherick.

Glyde Fosco ——

Fosco You need not to look so terrified. You are not ruined yet.

Glyde How do you know? How can you tell what that woman told her? (*He sits on the sofa*)

Fosco She did not tell her the secret — that I am convinced of ——

Glyde Why?

Fosco Because she has arranged to speak with them again. (*He hands the note to Glyde*) Read this. From her to Miss Halcombe.

Glyde (*after reading the note*) Anne Catherick is coming here tonight!

Fosco Yes.

Glyde Fosco, we must make sure of her, once and for all!

Fosco Of course.

Glyde But how do we do it? That's the thing. She's as cunning as a fox and she seems to sense me a mile off!

Fosco Do not perturb yourself. She will have no cause to be alarmed. When Anne Catherick walks into this room Miss Halcombe will be waiting for her.

Glyde Miss Halcombe! You said she'd gone to the station!

Fosco Fool, fool, fool! (*He moves to Countess* Fosco) Must I explain everything in the words of one syllable? Someone she *thinks* to be Miss Halcombe. (*He kisses his wife's hand*)

Glyde (*understanding*) Madame Fosco?

Fosco Precisely. My angel wife.

Countess Fosco hands Fosco a cigarette

Thank you, my cherub.

Countess Fosco gives him a light

Is she not adorable?

Glyde Well, what then?

Fosco When Anne Catherick has been conveyed back to her lunatic asylum, we will turn our attention to Lady Glyde.

Glyde (*rising*) Lady Glyde! (*He moves to sideboard and pours another drink*)

Fosco (*pausing to draw on his cigarette*) My friend, how much do you care for your wife? (*He sits on the* L *arm of the sofa*)

Glyde (*his glass clinking against the decanter*) What?

Fosco You heard me.

Glyde That's rather a downright question.

Fosco To which I should like a downright answer.

Glyde You've seen us together. She cares nothing for me. She's in love with a poverty-stricken drawing master.

Fosco And you care even less for her. How much have you with her at present?

Glyde You mean in money?

Fosco nods

Nothing but the interest of her eighty thousand.

Fosco Nothing more?

Glyde The reversion of the Fairlie estate when her uncle dies.

Fosco Ah. Yes, you have told me of him. But men of that sort live long and marry when you least expect it. So there is nothing more that comes to you from your wife?

Glyde Nothing — except in the event of her death.

Fosco Ah. Yes. Her death. When you would receive the entire eighty thousand pounds ... Yes ...

Glyde Now see here, Fosco, I don't know what's in your mind — at least, I think I do ——

Fosco Nonsense, you could never fathom such a mind as mine! Now, let us suppose — suppose, I say, your wife should die before the year is out ——

Glyde And I say drop it, Fosco! Drop it, do you hear? I'll have no hand in such a thing!

Fosco Who has mentioned anything? I speak of your wife's death as a possibility, that's all.

Glyde Never mind. With your looks and your questions you make my flesh creep. (*He sits on the sofa*)

Fosco (*chuckling*) Your flesh? Does flesh mean conscience in English?

Glyde Drop it, I tell you! Speak of some other way out of our difficulty — but not that!

Fosco (*taking out his watch*) Very well. (*He rises*) It is now a quarter to ten. We should be making preparations to receive our visitor. Eleanor, my love.

Countess Fosco (*rising*) Yes, Count.

Fosco (*moving* UL) And attend to Lady Glyde's door as you pass.

Countess Fosco goes out UL

(*Moving to the bell*) Now, my friend, I wish you to do something in which you are adept. (*He rings the bell*)

Glyde What's that?

Fosco I wish you to be rude to the good Mrs Vesey.

Glyde Rude? Why?

Fosco Do you need a reason? You do it so naturally.

Glyde (*rising*) By heaven, Fosco I stand a good deal from you ——

Fosco (*viciously*) You will stand as much as I choose!

Glyde draws back

But since you must have a reason. I wish the good soul upset so that the kind Fosco, whom she likes so much, may comfort her with a sedative. Lady Glyde will find her door locked when she goes to try and meet Anne Catherick, and I would prefer that she is unable to wake Mrs Vesey.

The sound of Mrs Vesey's approach can be heard, off

(*In response to the sound*) Now, my friend, do as I say, or I wash my hands of your affairs. (*He moves to the fireplace*)

Mrs Vesey enters UL, *arriving at a position between Fosco and Glyde*

Mrs Vesey (*to Glyde*) Did I hear the bell, sir?
Glyde (*after a glance of fury at Fosco; to Mrs Vesey*) Where the devil have you been? I rang five minutes ago.
Mrs Vesey I beg your pardon, sir. I was just retiring.
Glyde Retiring? You take things easily here, don't you?
Mrs Vesey I asked Lady Glyde if there was anything further ——
Glyde I'm the head of this household during Mr Fairlie's absence! Not Lady Glyde!
Mrs Vesey You were not here, Sir Percival. I understood that you were not expected back until the morning.
Glyde I see. So that's why things were so lax.
Mrs Vesey I hadn't realized they were, sir. But I will ask for your instructions in the future.
Glyde The future! You take things for granted, don't you? What makes you suppose I mean to have you in my household in the future?
Mrs Vesey But Lady Glyde said ——
Glyde What Lady Glyde said is neither here or there!
Fosco My friend, you will wound Mrs Vesey.
Glyde (*throwing Fosco a baleful look*) Mrs Vesey can take herself out of this house tomorrow morning!
Mrs Vesey Oh, sir!
Glyde Is that clear? I don't want to see your face again!
Mrs Vesey Yes, sir, quite clear. I will do as you say.

Fosco gestures over Mrs Vesey's back for Glyde to go. Glyde moves towards the door R

Sir Percival ——

Glyde (*pausing*) Well?

Mrs Vesey I am not often rude. I hope I shall never be so again. But I cannot leave without saying that I think you the basest gentleman I have ever met in my born days.

Fosco is highly amused

I know it's wicked to wish anybody dead, but for my dear Laura's sake, I wish you had died before you met her! I wish you were dead ... I wish ... Oh ... (*She breaks down*)

Glyde takes a step towards Mrs Vesey, but Fosco waves him away

Glyde exits R

Fosco (*moving to Mrs Vesey*) There, there, Mrs Vesey. Sit down. (*He brings her to the sofa*)

Mrs Vesey Not in your presence, sir!

Fosco Never mind that.

Mrs Vesey sits

There, now.

Mrs Vesey Thank you, indeed, Count, for trying to interpose.

Fosco Have you somewhere to go when you leave here?

Mrs Vesey No, sir, nowhere.

Fosco (*handing her a card*) Then take this address. It is a good hotel in London and not expensive. (*He produces his wallet*) And this as well. (*He hands Mrs Vesey some money from the wallet*) It will help you till you find another place.

Mrs Vesey Oh, sir, I couldn't.

Fosco Come — let Fosco make amends for the ill-manners of his friend.

Mrs Vesey Thank you, sir.

Fosco Now you shall have a little glass of wine to settle your nerves. (*He moves up to the sideboard*)

Mrs Vesey Oh, I never touch wine, sir — or very rarely.

Fosco turns his back to Mrs Vesey, pours a glass of wine and fumbles something over it — a sleeping draught

Fosco Then this shall be one of the rare occasions. (*He brings the glass to her*) Drink this, Mrs Vesey. It will make you feel better.

Mrs Vesey (*after drinking about half of the glass*) Thank you, Count. You're very kind.

Fosco I try to be, Mrs Vesey. Now, down with the rest.
Mrs Vesey (*drinking the rest*) Count, you will look after Laura, won't you?
(*She puts the glass down on the sofa table*)

Fosco leads Mrs Vesey to the UL *door*

Fosco Rest assured, Mrs Vesey. I am most concerned of all with Lady Glyde.
Sleep well.
Mrs Vesey Good-night, Count, and thank you.

Mrs Vesey exits UL

Fosco shakes with laughter

Glyde enters

Glyde (*looking round*) Has she gone?
Fosco Yes, she will be dead to the world the moment her head touches the
pillow. (*He laughs again*)
Glyde What's so funny?
Fosco You, my friend. You should have seen your face!
Glyde That was a rotten thing to make me do! I felt a complete blackguard.
Fosco I know. That's such a novelty, isn't it? But never mind, my friend,
she's not a witch — her curse won't stick.

Countess Fosco enters UL *in a dress, cap and shawl of Marion's*

(*Moving to her*) Ah, my love, you look splendid! (*To Glyde*) You see? Miss
Halcombe's dress and shawl, and if she sits here with the one lamp ——
(*He brings Countess Fosco* DL)
Glyde Yes, I see. I'm not an idiot. (*He moves to the sideboard and fills his
glass*)
Fosco (*to Countess* Fosco) The lights have been attended to?
Countess Fosco I lighted the lamps in our rooms as I went up, and
extinguished them as I came down.
Glyde Why all the trouble? Anne Catherick is mad. (*He drinks*)
Fosco I have only your word for that. I have never seen her. But one whose
reason is deranged may yet be astute enough to watch windows. Now she
will assume we have all retired. This lamp must go out — (*he blows out the
desk lamp*) and that ——

Glyde moves to another lamp

No, not yet. Let us complete all here. The flowers on the window table. So. (*He places the bowl of flowers on the sideboard*) Now, Eleanor, when we are gone, draw back the curtains that she may see them.

Glyde Where shall we be?

Fosco In the hall behind those doors.

Glyde Fosco, you don't think we can fail?

Fosco We shall not fail.

Glyde That woman said she was dying in the letter. By God, Fosco — if she's died and left a statement ——

Fosco Pull yourself together!

Glyde That's all very well for you! You've nothing at stake but a paltry ten thousand! I have everything! Do you think I want to live like you — an outcast — a parasite ——

Fosco snatches the glass from Glyde's hand, and dashes the contents into Glyde's face. Glyde gasps, staggers back and sits in the armchair

Fosco If it were not for the money I could wish myself well rid of you!

Glyde goes to speak

Don't bluster and don't threaten! Get to your post! Little is required of you, but do that little well!

Glyde, after a second's hesitation, rises and exits R

Now the other lamp. (*He blows out the other lamp*) You will sit here, my love, in the shadow, with your embroidery. (*He hands her Laura's embroidery*) And give me a minute before you draw back the curtains.

A faint knocking is heard, off

Ah, Lady Glyde has discovered her door is locked.

Countess Fosco Can she be heard outside? (*He sits* DL)

Fosco I think not. We must risk that. She will soon tire of it. (*He surveys his wife*) That is well, my angel. To crazy eyes you look just like Miss Halcombe.

Fosco kisses Countess Fosco's hand and exits UL

Countess Fosco waits a few seconds, then rises and draws back the curtains. She resumes her seat, her head down, sewing

The figure of Anne Catherick comes into view, passes the window and disappears

Countess Fosco is motionless save for her busy hands

Anne Catherick reappears and taps gently

Countess Fosco lays down her needlework, rises and opens the window. Anne Catherick slips in, her hand pressed to her side

Anne (*moving into the room*) I've been waiting so long. Is Miss Fairlie coming?

Countess Fosco shuts the windows with a snap, and turns

You're not Miss Halcombe! Who are you?

Countess Fosco advances

No — no! Let me out — let me out! (*She runs round the armchair to the window*)

Countess Fosco struggles with Anne, but Anne, with unexpected strength, thrusts her away. She runs the to door UL

Fosco appears in the doorway UL, *barring the way*

Anne turns to the windows

Glyde appears in the french windows

Anne screams terribly and sways. Glyde runs forward and catches her as she faints

Fosco Bring her to the sofa.

Glyde carries Anne to the sofa and lays her down on it

Some water, Eleanor.

Countess Fosco moves to the sideboard and pours a glass of water

(*To Glyde, coming to the sofa*) Put back her shawl. Give her air.

Glyde does as instructed. Countess Fosco stands behind the sofa with the glass. Fosco suddenly sees clearly the girl on the sofa and stares down at her

Fosco Glyde — have we made a mistake?
Glyde Mistake? What do you mean?
Fosco Is this — Anne Catherick?
Glyde Of course it's Anne Catherick. Why?
Fosco Is it possible two beings can be so alike?
Glyde Oh, didn't I ever tell you she bore a sickly resemblance to my wife? Pleasant for me, wasn't it, with two women of the same cast of countenance haunting me.
Fosco (*slowly*) It is more than a resemblance — it is an identical likeness.

Countess Fosco dabs Anne's forehead with water

Glyde Never mind that! Why doesn't she come round?

Fosco kneels and listens to Anne's heart

  Don't say she's going to die on us!
Fosco She *is* going to die — within a very few hours.
Glyde What!
Fosco Or I am no authority.
Glyde We must get her to the asylum quickly!
Fosco No!
Glyde We can't keep her here in this state!
Fosco (*smiling*) Oh, my friend, my friend, what a mercy it is you have Fosco to look after you. The end of all your troubles stares you in the face and you fail to see it. (*He rises*)
Glyde What are you talking about?
Fosco Here you have Lady Glyde at death's door on the sofa ——
Glyde Lady Glyde? (*He looks down at Anne*)
Fosco And upstairs, captive, is Anne Catherick.
Glyde (*suddenly understanding*) Fosco! Can we — dare we — do it?
Fosco Who is to prevent us? (*He sits on the sofa, lifts Anne's wrist and feels her pulse*) And within a very few hours, my friend, you will become the master of eighty thousand pounds! (*He smiles up at Glyde*)

The Curtain *falls*

ACT III

The same. Four months later

When the CURTAIN *rises, the sky is overcast. Marion, dressed in black, stands at the french windows looking out anxiously*

The clock chimes once. She looks at it, plainly tense. She turns back and reacts to suddenly seeing someone outside

Marion (*calling, low and urgently*) Mr Hartright — Mr Hartright, come this way, if you please!

Hartright enters on to the terrace and heads for the french windows

Is Mr Gilmore with you?
Hartright Yes, he's just behind me.
Marion (*leading the way into the room*) I expected you half an hour ago.
Hartright (*following her*) I know. I'm sorry. I went to look at — the grave.
Marion I see.
Hartright I'm not very good at expressing myself, Miss Halcombe, but I think you know how I feel for you in your bereavement.
Marion Yes, I do. Thank you.
Hartright I made a drawing of it. (*He produces a drawing*) It's only four months — yet already the cross is a little weather-stained —— (*He hands the drawing to Marion*)
Marion (*reading from the drawing*) "Sacred to the memory of Laura, Lady Glyde, who departed this life November 23rd, 1861, aged twenty-one years. (*She hands the drawing back to Hartright*) You loved her very much, didn't you?
Hartright Yes.

Marion looks at him sympathetically

Gilmore appears at the french windows

Gilmore Is this right? Am I to come in this way?

Marion Mr Gilmore! Yes, please.

Gilmore enters the room. Marion closes the windows

Gilmore (*taking off his coat*) Nasty damp day. Blowing up for a gale. (*He puts his hat and his coat on the desk chair*)

Marion Please speak softly. I don't want any of my uncle's servants to know that either of you is here.

Gilmore My dear Miss Halcombe, what is this mystery? First, both Hartright and I receive an urgent summons from you to come here, and now you say you don't even wish our presence to be known.

Marion (*sitting on the sofa*) I've something of the utmost importance to tell you. Sit down, please.

Gilmore sits in the armchair RC, *Hartright on the sofa*

Mr Gilmore, do you remember a day, four months ago, when I came to see you in London? You were ill, and I had to wait three days before I could see you.

Gilmore I remember. You told me of an infamous attempt by Sir Percival Glyde to obtain his wife's signature to a deed that would make him master of her entire fortune. I advised you to tell her not to sign on any account.

Marion And you know the sequel to my journey. When I finally reached home I was told my sister was dead and buried.

Gilmore Yes, most distressing thing. I'd no idea she was suffering from a disease of the heart.

Marion She was not!

Gilmore My dear Miss Halcombe, the doctor's report proved it.

Marion My sister was alive and well at that moment. Not here — but in an asylum!

Hartright Miss Halcombe!

Marion The woman who died and was buried in her place, was Anne Catherick!

Gilmore Do you know what you're saying?

Marion I know very well what I'm saying.

Gilmore But it's utterly fantastic!

Hartright Let her go on, Mr Gilmore! Go on, Miss Halcombe!

Marion Anne Catherick resembled my sister most strongly. Mr Hartright will bear me out in that.

Hartright Yes, indeed.

Marion She had warned Laura about Sir Percival Glyde before her marriage ——

Hartright That's so, Mr Gilmore.

Marion After they returned from Italy she came here again. Somehow she'd discovered that Laura was unhappy, and she wanted to tell her some secret of his life as a weapon she could use against him. The night I left for London, Laura was to have met her. What happened I don't know — except that I returned to be told that Laura was dead.

Gilmore (*rising*) Miss Halcombe, I know you believe what you're saying, but it's utterly absurd. There could be no possibility of another woman being substituted for Lady Glyde ——

Marion Why not? Her uncle was still away. There were no friends or relatives at the funeral — only Sir Percival and Count Fosco, both of whom stood to gain by Laura's death.

Gilmore And you suggest that this other woman, who strongly resembled your sister, most opportunely died at the right moment for them?

Marion Anne Catherick was dying. Whether she died naturally I'm not prepared to say. I know Count Fosco well enough to believe that nature may have been given some assistance.

Hartright And you think Miss Fairlie is alive and well at this moment?

Marion I *know* she is — because she's here.

Hartright Here?

Marion I brought her back from the asylum early this morning — while it was still dark.

Gilmore Miss Halcombe ——

Hartright How do you know all this? When did you discover it?

Marion Not for some time. My own suspicions were as nothing against the doctor's certificate and the words of her husband and Count Fosco. Then, a few days after he returned, my uncle told me that Sir Percival had written to say Anne Catherick had been traced and sent back to the Home. This seemed curious ... I knew how deathly ill she was ... I determined to go and see her ——

Hartright Yes?

Marion I was taken to a garden where she was walking with a nurse — and I came face to face with my own sister!

Gilmore Why, in heaven's name, didn't you come straight to me?

Marion What would have been the use? I had no proof. Her clothes were the clothes of Anne Catherick — her looks were identical ——

Hartright How did you get her away?

Marion I had a little money — about two hundred pounds. The nurse who had charge of Laura was under notice to leave. She was easily bribed. We caught the train here, and I've concealed her ever since.

Gilmore Then no-one has seen her yet? Not even Mr Fairlie.

Marion No. Only Mrs Vesey, whom I met in London, is in our confidence.

Hartright (*rising*) Miss Halcombe — may I see Laura?

Marion (*rising*) Yes, I want you to — only you must be prepared for a change.

Hartright In what way?

Marion She is now so like Anne Catherick, that even when I look at her myself I am afraid. (*She goes to the door* R *and beckons*)

Laura enters. She is dressed as Anne Catherick, and has her pallor and her marks of suffering

Hartright makes a movement towards Laura, then stops. Gilmore stands rigid. Then Hartright moves again

Hartright (*holding out his hands*) Lady Glyde!

Laura You know me? (*She runs to Hartright*) You really know me? You're not pretending?

Hartright No. I could never forget you.

Laura breaks down

Don't — don't, please.

Laura sits on the sofa. Hartright sits by her

Laura I'm sorry. I know I'm so altered, but it was so dreadful in that place. I tried to tell them who I was, but they wouldn't listen to me — I tried and tried ——

Hartright Don't speak of it. That's all over now.

Laura You won't let them take me back?

Hartright They can't take you back now we know who you are.

Marion I wish that were true, Mr Hartright.

Hartright What?

Marion Ask Mr Gilmore.

Hartright Mr Gilmore, they can't take her back — can they?

Gilmore I'm very much afraid that they can.

Hartright But this is Lady Glyde! You know this is Lady Glyde!

Gilmore Yes, I know this is Laura. (*He moves to Laura and kisses her hand*) My dear, forgive an old man's momentary perplexity. I rejoice to see you restored to us.

Hartright Well, then ——

Gilmore The fact remains, Mr Hartright, that in law we haven't the shadow of a case!

Hartright That's preposterous! Why, she's here, in her own home! Everything is known to her. She could describe in detail every incident of her life ——

Gilmore Am I right in assuming, Miss Halcombe, that Anne Catherick also knew Limmeridge Hall?

Marion Yes, she was here as a child in my mother's time.

Gilmore You see, Mr Hartright, what we're up against. Sir Percival would simply retort that we were trying to cheat him of Lady Glyde's fortune by promoting an impostor.

Hartright But her own uncle is here! (*Rising*) Surely his recognition would help? He can have no ulterior motive.

Gilmore Yes, Mr Fairlie's recognition would help a great deal. Do you think I could see him, Miss Halcombe?

Marion Yes, of course. I'll come with you.

Gilmore goes out UL

Stay with Laura, Mr Hartright. I've locked the windows and Mrs Vesey has orders to allow no-one in here.

Hartright Miss Halcombe — is there a stable boy — or anyone here you can trust?

Marion Yes, there's Jem. Why?

Hartright Tell him to go to the station and report back here the moment the London train comes in.

Marion I understand. I'll do that, Mr Hartright.

Marion exits UL

Laura (*rising*) You think — my husband and Count Fosco will be on it?

Hartright I'm sure of it. They must know of your escape by now.

Laura turns away

Miss Fairlie — Laura —— (*Moving to her*) I want with all my heart to help you. Could you bear to tell me what happened the night you were to have met Anne Catherick?

Laura Yes, of course. (*She sits in the armchair*)

Hartright sits on the sofa

Marion had gone to London. I went early to my room. I intended to come down again when everybody was in bed. Just before ten o'clock I heard footsteps in the corridor and the sound of doors closing.

Hartright They were retiring?

Laura That's what I thought. I waited a little longer. Then I crept towards the door and tried to open it. It was locked!

Hartright Locked!

Laura I realized then that they'd discovered about Anne Catherick and were going to trap her.

Hartright Could you hear anything?

Laura Not at first. All was quiet. Then — suddenly — I heard a scream of terror ——

Hartright A woman's scream?

Laura Yes. Then everything was quiet again — until …

Hartright Yes?

Laura I heard footsteps coming towards my room. I was terrified — there was nowhere for me to run or hide. The key was turned in the door and my husband stood there. Fosco was behind him. They came towards me. Something was pressed over my face and I lost consciousness. When I came to I was in a strange room — in these clothes — and people were calling me Anne Catherick.

Hartright (*rising*) There is a way out of this! There must be!

Laura My position doesn't matter — I'd forfeit it gladly, so long as they won't take me back!

Hartright They shall never take you back while I'm here. (*He moves to her*)

Laura (*rising*) You *will* stay with me?

Hartright (*taking her hands*) Always, my dearest — always.

They look at each other. Then he draws her close and holds her

Marion enters UL

Marion Mr Fairlie is coming. Laura, you'd better stay in there until I call you. (*She opens the door* R)

Hartright Have you prepared him?

Marion As far as was possible.

Fairlie's voice is heard, off

Laura!

Laura exits R

Marion closes the door and moves to the fireplace

Mr Fairlie (*off*) Don't jolt me, Gilmore! I have little enough peace as it is, but don't jolt me!

Mr Fairlie is wheeled in UL *by Gilmore. He sees Hartright*

Good gracious, do my eyes deceive me?

Hartright Good-evening, Mr Fairlie.

Mr Fairlie It *is* that Hartright person. Have you the impertinence to enter my house again, after the unceremonious way you left it?

Hartright I'm here to see a great injustice righted.

Mr Fairlie Louis! Where is Louis? I want Louis!

Gilmore You can't have him.

Mr Fairlie But I can't exist without Louis! I need my smelling salts. I can smell horrible trains!

Gilmore Mr Fairlie, did you listen to one word we said to you?

Mr Fairlie Of course I listened. I was obliged to listen, since I had no means of getting out of the room. Though why you must come and worry me with this cock and bull story about my niece being substituted in her grave for another woman, I can't imagine.

Gilmore Your niece is alive!

Mr Fairlie Rubbish! I read her obituary in *The Times* myself. Believe me, Gilmore, you've been taken in by this maniac Glyde warned me about.

Hartright That is a lie!

Mr Fairlie I beg your pardon? It's the drawing master speaking, I believe?

Hartright (*turning to Marion*) Miss Halcombe, you must show Laura to him. There's no other way of convincing him.

Marion looks at Gilmore, who nods. Marion opens the door R

Marion Laura, come in.

Laura enters

Mr Fairlie stares at her

Laura (*coming in a little way*) Uncle, you know me, don't you? I'm Laura. It's true what you've heard. They shut me up for months in a dreadful place. I couldn't write or let you know what had become of me ——

Mr Fairlie How did this woman get here?

Laura Uncle!

Marion I got Laura away from the Home last night ——

Mr Fairlie The Home? This mental asylum?

Laura Oh, Uncle, don't you see —— (*She moves nearer to Mr Fairlie*)

Mr Fairlie Keep her away from me! Why, this — this creature must be reeking with germs! I shall be prostrate tomorrow!

Gilmore Good God, man, forget yourself for a moment! This is your niece returned from the grave!

Mr Fairlie This is not my niece! I told you you'd been imposed upon! I never saw this woman before in my life!

Marion Uncle, this *is* Laura! How can you look on her and deny it?

Mr Fairlie I say she is not Laura! Did Laura dress like that? Did Laura have a pinched white face and shadows under her eyes? An imposition, plainly!

Hartright moves DL

Laura (*kneeling*) Oh, Uncle, I know I've changed, but can't you imagine what I've been through? Let me try and convince you, please! Ask me questions — ask me anything about myself — about this house — about my life before I was married! I can answer anything!

Mr Fairlie Oh, yes, I've no doubt they've primed you! How much money have you been offered if you succeed in this deception ——

Laura Uncle! (*She rises*)

Gilmore Mr Fairlie!

Mr Fairlie (*propelling his chair* DC) — and you — you penniless hack — (*to Hartright*) how much are you getting to set her up in my niece's place?

Laura sobs. Marion goes to her

Oh, it was a pretty plot, but I'm not deceived. Stand out of my way, sir! (*He attempts to wheel his chair off*)

Hartright stands before Mr Fairlie

Hartright Not yet. You called me a penniless hack, Mr Fairlie. Maybe I am, but I thank God I'm not like you with all your money — a selfish, heartless wretch!

Mr Fairlie Gilmore, he's calling me names!

Hartright If you were half a man I'd knock you down — not for what you said to me, but for the things you've said to a helpless woman who's suffered more in four months than you have in all your born days!

Mr Fairlie Don't you dare offer me violence! My heart is weak! (*He backs his chair away*)

Hartright I'm not going to offer you violence. Can you walk?

Mr Fairlie What?

Hartright Can he walk, Miss Halcombe?

Marion A little — when he tries.

Hartright Get up!

Mr Fairlie That's not true! I can't walk! I'm as helpless as a child!

Hartright Get up!

Hartright tips Mr Fairlie out of his chair

Now walk back to your room! Go on, walk!

Mr Fairlie totters up, grasping the furniture piece by piece

Mr Fairlie My legs are failing me!

Hartright (*following him*) Good! Then crawl! Crawl to your room! Creep
to it! And make haste before my temper gets the better of me!

Mr Fairlie (*on his hands and knees*) Don't think you've heard the last of this!
I shall send Louis for the constables!

Hartright Do so, and I'll break your neck! I'd hang willingly for that
pleasure!

Mr Fairlie exits UL

(*Hurling the chair after Mr Fairlie*) And take your go-cart with you! (*He
slams the door*)

Gilmore That wasn't wise, Mr Hartright, but I understand your feelings.
Laura, you must make ready to leave with me.

Hartright Leave? Why must she go?

Gilmore Because the hunt must be out for her already, and the first place
Glyde and Fosco will look for her is here.

Laura What's going to become of me? Shall I always be moving on and on
in hiding?

Gilmore We'll try and get you out of the country, my dear. Miss Halcombe
will go with you.

Marion Of course.

Laura But how shall we live? I have nothing.

Hartright Let me take care of that. I can work for all of us.

Marion And I can work, too. I'll help Mr Hartright. Let's make ready to go,
Laura. We've nothing to stay for here.

Marion leads Laura UR. *Laura and Marion exit* R

Hartright This is damnable! That poor girl driven from her home by these
scoundrels!

The church clock strikes six, off

Gilmore (*looking at his watch*) Six o'clock by Old Welmington Church and
my watch, and the London train comes in at seven. We have one hour, Mr
Hartright, in which to get those girls away.

Hartright Or to prove that Laura is Lady Glyde. (*He moves to the window*)
Old Welmington Church … I wonder why Glyde disliked it to much? Mr
Gilmore, have we been forgetting something all along?

Gilmore For instance?

Hartright What was Glyde's motive for wanting Laura out of the way?

Gilmore That's obvious. The money. (*He sits in the armchair*)

Hartright But was it his only reason? Did Miss Halcombe show you a copy of the letter Anne Catherick wrote?

Gilmore Oh, you mean that nonsense about his having a secret?

Hartright Is it nonsense? Remember, the very fact that Anne Catherick knew it was sufficient to make Glyde have her put away. If only we could find it out!

Gilmore But Anne Catherick is dead, and only Anne Catherick knew it.

Hartright No! There's somebody else who knows it! Of course!

Gilmore Who?

Hartright Anne Catherick's mother! Anne overheard them talking about it. And she lives in this village, Gilmore. I'm going to see her!

Gilmore You're wasting time, and we've very little.

Hartright It's not ten minutes away. I remember the place from the last time I was here. It's worth a try, Gilmore. (*He moves to the french windows and unlocks them*)

At the same moment, Mrs Vesey enters UL

Mrs Vesey Mr Gilmore, there's a person here who says she must see Miss Halcombe.

Gilmore Who is it?

Mrs Vesey She gave her name as Mrs Catherick.

Hartright Mrs Catherick! Gilmore!

Gilmore (*rising*) Show her in here, Mrs Vesey.

Mrs Vesey goes

Hartright Gilmore, this is providential!

Gilmore I don't like it. Be careful.

Hartright But ——

Gilmore We've no idea how much this woman knows. She may even be aware of the substitution. If she is, then she's a very dangerous enemy.

Mrs Vesey enters UL

Mrs Vesey (*announcing*) Mrs Catherick, sir.

Mrs Catherick enters. She is a grim-featured woman of middle age. Mrs Vesey goes

Mrs Catherick (*stopping at the door*) I asked to see Miss Halcombe.

Gilmore Miss Halcombe is engaged. I am her solicitor. You may state your business to me.

Mrs Catherick (*moving* c) And if I do not choose?

Gilmore Then it must remain unspoken. Miss Halcombe is unacquainted with you, so it can hardly be for her ears alone.

Mrs Catherick Very well.

Hartright Won't you sit down?

Mrs Catherick (*staring at Hartright*) Yes — if I wish to. (*To Gilmore*) I received news from the asylum that my daughter had escaped again. The superintendent stated that Miss Halcombe was the last person to speak with her. I wondered if she might be able to throw some light on her disappearance. (*She sits on the sofa*)

Gilmore From a natural interest in your daughter's welfare, I presume?

Mrs Catherick No. I don't like idiots. I don't want her at large.

Hartright Why? Because she might talk?

Mrs Catherick (*with a scornful laugh*) Talk! Her? What could she talk about?

Hartright Something which Sir Percival Glyde might prefer to keep unknown.

Mrs Catherick I don't know what you mean. If you can give me no news of my daughter I shall go. (*She rises*)

Hartright But I can give you news of your daughter.

Mrs Catherick Well?

Hartright She is dead.

Mrs Catherick That is certain?

Hartright Yes.

Mrs Catherick Then I am glad to hear it.

Gilmore Glad! Great heavens, have you no feelings?

Mrs Catherick Feelings! Do you think I ever had any love for her? A maniac I was ashamed to have borne? I'm glad she's dead — glad, do you hear? I never saw her face without wanting to spit in it!

Hartright Aren't you likely to be the loser now she's dead?

Mrs Catherick Must you talk in riddles?

Hartright Will Sir Percival Glyde continue to send you money now she's out of the way?

Mrs Catherick turns to the door. Hartright bars her way

Hartright He does send you money, doesn't he, to buy your silence?

Mrs Catherick Let me pass!

Hartright But you're not safe, you know. Before she died your daughter told the secret to Lady Glyde!

Mrs Catherick What!

Hartright There'll be no more help from Glyde, so you may as well tell us everything!

Mrs Catherick You're lying! I can see you're lying! You know nothing. You're trying to trap me!

Hartright Are you so afraid of him?

Mrs Catherick Afraid — of *him*! Do I look as if I were afraid of Glyde?

Hartright Why shouldn't you be? He's a powerful man — a baronet — the descendant of a great family ——

Mrs Catherick laughs scornfully

Why do you laugh?

Mrs Catherick Oh, yes, a baronet — a powerful man — the descendant of a great family. Bah, you make me tired! You know nothing and you'll learn nothing from me. If Lady Glyde knows the secret ask *her*! (*She moves to go*)

Hartright Mrs Catherick, wait. Let me appeal to you. I'm trying to help right a great injustice. By telling the truth you can help someone who is very near and dear to me from a life that must be worse than your own daughter's ...

Mrs Catherick What do I care for anyone who's near and dear to you? Nobody cared for me! I was pursued by the tongues of slander when I'd done no wrong. A few scandalmongers saw me once in the vestry of the church with Glyde and concluded I was a light woman. *I've* suffered enough, I can tell you!

Hartright Why were you in the vestry of the church?

Mrs Catherick Why shouldn't I be? My husband was parish clerk of Old Welmington.

Hartright (*looking at Gilmore*) Old Welmington.

Mrs Catherick When my husband died they tried to drive me from the village, but I wouldn't go. I was innocent and I determined to stay. Now there is nobody more respected here than I am. Let this person who you say is near and dear to you, live it down as I did! Find out what you want in your own way! You'll get no help from me!

Laura enters R

Mrs Catherick sees Laura and staggers back

Hartright Mrs Catherick ——

Mrs Catherick You told me she was dead! Why did you tell me she was dead?

Hartright This is not your daughter. This is Lady Glyde.

Mrs Catherick (*staring at Laura*) Lady Glyde! *Lady Glyde!*

Mrs Catherick exits quickly UL

Marion enters R

Hartright Wait! She mustn't go! (*He heads for the door* UL)
Gilmore (*stopping Hartright*) You can't keep her here by force! What are you doing?
Laura Was that Mrs Catherick?
Gilmore Yes. It was unfortunate she saw you. She's bound to meet Sir Percival at the station and tell him you're here. You must go at once.
Hartright No, not yet! Gilmore, she told us something!
Gilmore She told us nothing! (*Moving to Laura*) Laura ——
Hartright She said she met Glyde in the vestry of the church ——
Gilmore What of it?
Hartright I'm more and more convinced Old Welmington Church has something to do with the mystery … The vestry of a church … What does that mean to you, Gilmore?
Gilmore A place where you keep the parish records, I suppose.
Hartright Yes — births, marriages and deaths. Could it be possible that Glyde was married before, and his second marriage was a bigamous one?
Gilmore This is far-fetched, Mr Hartright!
Hartright Perhaps — but there is something — or why should he be so frightened?
Marion Could we search the records of Old Welmington Church?
Hartright Why not?
Gilmore Mr Hartright ——
Hartright We must try everything!
Gilmore Very well, if you insist.

Hartright moves UL

No, no, let *me* go. I'm the safest person to be seen outside this house. (*He moves to the french windows*) Laura, my dear, don't build on this. I can't hold out any hope we may be right.

Gilmore takes up his hat and coat and exits through the french windows

The clock strikes the half-hour, off

Laura (*moving to the windows*) Half-past six. They'll be here by seven.
Hartright They shan't take you, my dearest. I won't let them. I'm convinced we're on the right track at last.
Marion Will it take long for Mr Gilmore to search the records?

Hartright Long enough. If only we had that old copy he once told me about.

Marion What old copy?

Hartright Apparently one of the other Mr Fairlie's friends kept a copy of the marriage register. It was his hobby.

Marion Old Mr Wansborough?

Hartright Yes, I think that was the name.

Marion But I believe that copy may be here!

Laura | *(together)* | Marion!
Hartright | | Here!

Marion Old Mr Wansborough left his library to my father. It might be among them!

Hartright Can I help you look?

Marion No, if it's here at all, I know what it looks like.

Marion exits R

Laura Do you really think it will solve the mystery?

Hartright I don't know. I can only hope and pray that it does.

There is a tap at the door UL

Yes?

Mrs Vesey enters

Mrs Vesey Mr Hartright, Jem has come back from the station ——

Hartright I told him not to leave until the London train came in!

Mrs Vesey It came in half an hour ago. The service has been altered!

Hartright Were Glyde and Fosco on it?

Mrs Vesey Yes. Jem says they took the station cab and drove off towards the village.

Hartright I see ... Thank you, Mrs Vesey.

Mrs Vesey exits

Laura Will they have gone to see Mrs Catherick?

Hartright I'm afraid so.

Laura But she'll tell them she saw me here! (*She sits on the sofa*)

Hartright Yes.

Laura turns away

(*Sitting by Laura*) We haven't lost the game yet, Laura — only we've less time than we thought. We may have to make ready to leave very soon.

Marion enters R *carrying a large volume*

Marion I found it!
Hartright (*rising*) Miss Halcombe!
Marion What date do we want? (*She moves to the armchair and sits*)
Hartright (*moving to her*) What year did Glyde leave Old Welmington?
Marion The year his parents died. 1841.
Hartright Then 1840 — or thereabouts.
Marion (*turning the pages*) 1840 — ah, here we are. (*She runs her finger down the page*) Kane — Albright — Jackson ——
Hartright Wilmer — James — Hobson — no.
Marion (*turning the page*) Try 1839.
Hartright 1839. (*He runs his finger down the page*) No.
Marion 1842? He might have come back.
Hartright (*looking*) No.
Laura (*rising*) Oh, Marion, it's hopeless!
Marion The year before?
Hartright (*looking*) No … I'm sorry, Laura … I was so sure I was on the right track.

Mr Gilmore enters through the french windows, panting. There is straw clinging to his coat

Marion Mr Gilmore ——
Gilmore Let me sit down. (*He sits in the desk chair*) I haven't run so fast in years!
Hartright You've found something?
Gilmore Found something? No! If ever there was a wild goose chase, that was. No, the reason I ran was that I'd barely copied this when who should come in but Sir Percival Glyde! (*He produces a piece of paper, and puts it on the desk*)
Hartright Into the church?
Gilmore Not only the church — the vestry.
Marion Did he see you?
Gilmore I'm afraid he did. I had the devil's own job to get out. The confounded lock stuck.
Hartright You say you found nothing?
Gilmore Nothing at all. If Glyde married secretly he didn't do it at Old Welmington.
Marion Then why did he go straight into the vestry?
Gilmore My dear young lady, if we knew that we wouldn't be asking ourselves all these questions. (*He brushes himself down*) Confound this straw! They're repairing the woodwork, and the place is filled with old wood and packing cases.

Hartright (*taking up Gilmore's paper*) What's this you've copied?

Gilmore Oh, the record of his parents' marriage. I thought you might get a bee in your bonnet about that, and I didn't relish another visit.

Hartright Could Anne Catherick have been his illegitimate daughter, and he put her away to keep her quiet?

Gilmore My dear young man, if everybody placed their illegitimate children in asylums there'd be no room for the insane. Besides, it's not a criminal offence, and from Glyde's anxiety to hide it, it must be something which places him within reach of the law.

Hartright Yes, that's true. (*He lays the paper on the table by the armchair*)

Gilmore (*to Laura*) I'm going up to Mr Fairlie, my dear.

Laura moves up to Gilmore

I shall tell him you're leaving the country, and try to persuade him to take no action about Mr Hartright's unfortunate assault. Keep a stout heart, my dear. We shall get you away.

Gilmore exits UL

Hartright I'm afraid this is the end, Laura. We're defeated.

Laura (*moving to the french windows*) And yet Sir Percival didn't come *here* first — he drove straight to the church.

Hartright *And* entered the vestry. Somehow I still believe the solution to the mystery lies in those pages.

Marion picks up Gilmore's page and compares it with the pages of the register

Laura What else can we look for?

Hartright I don't know, Laura. I don't know.

Marion (*suddenly*) Mr Hartright!

Hartright What is it?

Laura You've found something?

Laura and Hartright move to Marion

Marion I'm not sure. (*She hands Gilmore's paper to Hartright*) Look at that carefully, Mr Hartright.

Hartright It's the record of the marriage of Glyde's parents Gilmore copied from the parish register.

Marion You notice the date?

Hartright September the 9th, 1813.

Marion Now look at a corresponding date in here.
Hartright (*looking*) Good God!
Laura What is it? What *is* it?
Hartright There's no record of this marriage here at all!
Laura No record!
Marion Look at this page again, Mr Hartright. Remember this is an exact facsimile of the parish register. Do you see the small space left between the preceding and the following marriages?
Hartright Marion, you've found it!
Laura I still don't understand.
Hartright (*holding up Gilmore's paper*) This entry in the parish register was forged!
Laura Forged!
Hartright Glyde's parents were never married! He forged this entry later. He has no more claim to the baronetcy he holds than I have! It's the end of the search, my dearest. You're safe now. He can't touch you any more!

Fosco appears in the french windows and leans against the frame. He carries a slim cane — a sword stick

Fosco I regret to disillusion you, Mr Hartright.

Hartright, Laura and Marion turn

You *are* Mr Hartright, are you not?
Marion (*rising*) Count Fosco!

Laura shrinks back DR

Fosco I hope you are well, Miss Halcombe. And Lady Glyde here, too. How opportune.

Fosco moves into the room. Hartright makes a movement UR *towards him and Fosco draws the sword from his sword stick. Marion puts the book down on the table and moves to Laura*

Fosco No — no nearer, Mr Hartright, if you please. I don't wish there to be any unpleasantness.
Hartright I advise you to get clear while you can. We've all the proofs of your rascality in our hands.
Fosco Not quite, Mr Hartright. I did a little eavesdropping before I showed myself, so I am quite aware of all you know. You will need the parish register before you can prove anything, I fancy.

Hartright It's only a matter of minutes to obtain that.

Fosco True. But unfortunately Glyde has gone before you. There will be a little fire in the vestry — nothing much, you understand, but sufficient to destroy some valuable records.

Marion Destroy!

Fosco Such a pity after your neat little piece of deduction.

Hartright Then we were right?

Fosco Quite right. Glyde is illegitimate. So when a marriage certificate was demanded in order to prove his title to the baronetcy, he was obliged to resort to forgery.

Hartright And Mrs Catherick admitted him to the vestry?

Fosco (*nodding and smiling*) For which he paid her ever after. See how simple it all is when one knows!

A red light — as from a fire — is seen outside the window. Fosco glances towards it

Fosco Ah, there it goes now! With this wind fanning it, I fear nothing can save the vestry.

Hartright You know there's a penalty for destroying a marriage register?

Fosco (*smiling and shaking his head*) There is no penalty for an accidental fire. And then we shall take Lady Glyde back to the nice home we have found for her, where you, Mr Hartright, will be unable to reach her.

Hartright You damned scoundrel!

Mrs Vesey runs in UL

Mrs Vesey Mr Hartright — the vestry is on fire — and there's somebody locked in there!

Fosco What!

Hartright Locked in!

Mrs Vesey They say a gentleman went in and locked the door behind him! Now he can't get out! He's calling for help! It's horrible!

Hartright That lock — Gilmore said it stuck! And the vestry is full of straw and packing cases!

Marion Can't they break down the doors?

Mrs Vesey They've tried — they're too strong! No-one can reach him!

Laura (*sitting*) Oh, how dreadful!

Marion Send all the help you can from the house, Mrs Vesey.

Mrs Vesey nods and exits UL

Fosco Mr Hartright, I will bargain with you, Glyde is dead — or so nearly dead as makes no matter.

Hartright Are you human? You were his friend!

Fosco (*shrugging*) What is friendship? A feeling — no more. You want Lady Glyde's restoration to her name and fortune — is that not so?

Hartright Her name, certainly.

Fosco Then give me ten thousand pounds and forty-eight hours to get away, and I will give you a complete statement as to how the substitution was effected.

Hartright Give me five minutes without that sword stick, and I'll undertake to beat the truth out of you!

Fosco Bah. I hate the heroics! (*Moving to Laura*) Lady Glyde. I appeal to you. You can spare ten thousand pounds out of your eighty for poor Fosco?

Laura (*after a moment*) Very well.

Fosco I salute the sensible lady. I will write to you where our mutual exchange shall be effected, and then — to Italy — to sunshine — to the Villa Fosco! Fosco returns to the land of his fathers! (*He salutes them all elaborately*) Miss Halcombe — Lady Glyde — Mr Hartright — farewell!

Fosco exits through the french windows

Marion Laura!

Laura Oh, Marion! (*She rises and runs to Marion*) To be known again — and acknowledged!

They embrace

Hartright (*smiling*) Mr Fairlie will have to be told. Poor Mr Fairlie. Two shocks in one day.

Marion Let me tell him!

Laura Marion, be kind!

Marion Kind! I hope it prostrates him for a month!

Marion exits UL

Hartright moves to Laura, puts his arm about her and walks with her to the windows

Hartright The fire is dying down. The ashes will be blowing over the grave of Anne Catherick.

Laura What was the inscription on the stone? I've never seen it.

Hartright (*taking his drawing from his pocket*) Read it.

Laura (*taking the drawing and reading from it*) "Sacred to the memory of Laura, Lady Glyde, who departed this life November 23rd, 1861 ——"

Hartright And who returned to life this 15th day of March, 1862 — to life — to love — and to liberty.

Hartright takes the drawing from Laura, tears it across and lets the pieces fall. Then he takes her in his arms and they kiss, as ——

—— the CURTAIN *falls*

FURNITURE AND PROPERTY LIST

ACT I
Scene 1

On stage: Two small chairs
Footwarmer
Fireplace. *Above it*: mirror. *On mantelpiece*: clock. *Beside it*: fire-irons, bellows
Armchair
Two small tables
Sideboard. *On it*: lamp, decanter of sherry, wine decanter, jug of water, glasses, biscuits, corkscrew
Screen
Desk. *On it*: lamp, pens, inkstand, notepaper, blotting paper, sealing-wax, two sketch-books, paperweight
Desk chair
Sofa
Occasional table
Small footstool

Windows and curtains open

Off stage: Fumigating spray (**Louis**)
Invalid chair with portfolio of drawings, fan (**Mr Fairlie**)
Slippers (**Mrs Vesey**)
Letter (**Marion**)

Personal: **Marion**: reticule containing notecase with money in it

Scene 2

Set: Drawing, and drawing implements, for **Hartright**

Strike: Sketch-books

Off stage: Letter (**Anne**)

Personal: **Gilmore**: document
Louis: vial of smelling salts
Marion: letter

ACT II
SCENE 1

Re-set:	Sofa C, small table in front of it, armchair further DS
Set:	**Hartright**'s drawing in frame over fireplace
Strike:	Drawing implements, screen, footstool, footwarmer
Off stage:	Tray of tea things including plate of small cakes (**Marion**) Bag (**Mrs Vesey**) Teapot (**Mrs Vesey**) Letter (**Mrs Vesey**) Bottles of wine (**Glyde** and **Fosco**)
Personal:	**Countess Fosco**: little box containing cigarette-making materials and matches (carried throughout) **Glyde**: document

SCENE 2

Re-set:	Sofa, small table and armchair to previous positions French windows open
Set:	Screen, footstool, footwarmer Tray of coffee cups, pot, milk jug, sugar etc. on sofa table Bowl of flowers on table L Embroidery on sofa arm
Strike:	Tea things, used wine glasses
Off stage:	Note (**Marion**) Note (**Countess Fosco**)
Personal:	**Fosco**: card, wallet with money

ACT III

Strike:	Coffee things, bowl of flowers, embroidery
Off stage:	Large volume (**Marion**)
Personal:	**Hartright**: drawing **Gilmore**: piece of paper **Fosco**: sword stick

LIGHTING PLOT

Practical fittings required: fire effect in grate, lamps
One interior with room and exterior backings. The same throughout

ACT I, SCENE 1

To open: General interior and exterior lighting with summer effect, and fire effect in grate

Cue 1	**Mrs Vesey** blows up the fire with the bellows	(Page 5)
	Increase fire effect in grate; fade slightly as scene progresses	
Cue 2	**Hartright** closes the curtains	(Page 5)
	Dim interior lighting	
Cue 3	**Hartright** opens the curtains	(Page 7)
	Increase interior lighting	
Cue 4	**Hartright** closes the curtains	(Page 7)
	Dim interior lighting	
Cue 5	**Laura** opens the curtains	(Page 9)
	Increase interior lighting	
Cue 6	**Mrs Vesey** blows up the fire with the bellows	(Page 23)
	Increase fire effect in grate	

ACT I, SCENE 2

To open: General interior and exterior lighting with summer effect, and fire effect in grate; exterior lighting fades slowly through scene

Cue 7	**Mrs Vesey** lights the sideboard lamp	(Page 14)
	Bring up sideboard lamp and follow spot	
Cue 8	**Hartright** lights desk lamp	(Page 14)
	Bring up desk lamp and covering spot	

ACT II, Scene 1

To open: General interior and exterior lighting with winter afternoon effect, and fire effect in grate

No cues

ACT II, Scene 2

To open: General interior and exterior lighting with winter evening effect, fire effect in grate, lamps lit with covering spots

| *Cue* 9 | **Fosco** blows out desk lamp | (Page 55) |
| | *Cut desk lamp and covering spot* | |

| *Cue* 10 | **Fosco** blows out sideboard lamp | (Page 56) |
| | *Cut sideboard lamp and covering spot* | |

ACT III

To open: General interior and exterior lighting with overcast spring effect

| *Cue* 11 | **Fosco**: " … when one knows!" | (Page 76) |
| | *Red light on exterior backing as from a fire* | |

EFFECTS PLOT

ACT I

Cue 1   **Laura**: "In the autumn."   (Page 9)
        Gong

Cue 2   **Mrs Vesey**: "But he expressly said ——"   (Page 11)
        Door slam

Cue 3   **Marion** enters UL   (Page 12)
        Door slam

Cue 4   **Laura**: " … one of you."   (Page 14)
        Gong

ACT II

Cue 5   **Fosco**: " … draw back the curtains."   (Page 56)
        Faint knocking

ACT III

Cue 6   When ready   (Page 59)
        Clock chimes once

Cue 7   **Hartright**: " … her home by these scoundrels!"   (Page 67)
        Church clock strikes six

Cue 8   **Gilmore** exits   (Page 71)
        Church clock strikes half-past six